Need to Manage a Virtual Team?

Theory and Practice in a Nutshell.

by

Dr. Beat Buhlmann

Zug, Switzerland

December 2006

Bibliografische Information Der Deutschen Bibliothek
Die Deutsche Bibliothek verzeichnet diese Publikation in der Deutschen
Nationalbibliografie; detaillierte bibliografische Daten sind im Internet über
http://dnb.ddb.de abrufbar.
1. Aufl. - Göttingen : Cuvillier, 2006
   Zugl.: Adelaide, Univ., Diss., 2006

   ISBN 10: 3-86727-072-4
   ISBN 13: 978-3-86727-072-4

© CUVILLIER VERLAG, Göttingen 2006
   Nonnenstieg 8, 37075 Göttingen
   Telefon: 0551-54724-0
   Telefax: 0551-54724-21
   www.cuvillier.de

1. Auflage, 2006
Gedruckt auf säurefreiem Papier

   ISBN 10: 3-86727-072-4
   ISBN 13: 978-3-86727-072-4

Home is where the heart is.

How to Read this Book

This book is based on a research project for a professional doctorate (DBA), trying to address and cover the needs of both researchers and practitioners. Students and researchers may read it as usual from the beginning. Considering the scarce time of people working in fast-paced real-world environments, they may directly start with Chapter 5 as it provides specifically framed managerial recommendations, aimed at being easily accessible without lengthy reading times. For those who then are also interested in better understanding the background and the connections behind the recommendations, the previous chapters provide an account of the results and key findings of the research itself in more depth.

Enjoy!

☺

Table of Contents

List of Figures

List of Tables

Summary

In the rapidly changing and globalised business environment of the IT industry, virtual teams represent an emerging and increasingly prevalent work form. This dissertation seeks to understand what makes for the successful management of virtual teams, conducting a field study in the marketing department of an international IT company in Europe (henceforth called XYZ Europe). Since this dissertation is meant to provide something valuable about virtual teams in general, as well as something for XYZ Europe in particular, a mixed methodology approach was chosen. A research framework involving observation and semi-structured interviews was therefore instituted, with data collection and analysis based on ethnographic approaches. Eighteen virtual team members of XYZ Europe were observed and interviewed. Afterwards, the data were analysed and interpreted with the help of qualitative analysis software (NVivo). Subsequently, I compared my findings with those of the literature reviewed. From a theory point of view, a gap in the literature, the need for testing the theoretical assumptions against real-life conditions, could be addressed. Moreover, current models of virtual teams were applied in XYZ Europe's real-world environment and altered where needed. In addition, this study questions whether trust can be 'built' (as the largely positivist literature about virtual teams seems to suggest), or whether it needs to be earned. Finally, advantages and drawbacks associated with virtual teams are identified, and practical approaches for managing virtual teams in areas like recruitment, communication, or increasing trust are suggested. From a practical view point, acting virtual team managers can easily access the specifically highlighted managerial recommendations without reading for a long time, a relevant requirement in a fast-paced industry. For those who are also interested in better understanding the connections behind the suggestions, Chapter 4 provides an account of the results and key findings of the research itself in more depth.

SUMMARY

Chapter 1: Introduction and Rationale

Overview

It is commonly argued that globalization of trade and production, new consumer needs and behaviours, changes in the markets, as well as technological innovations demand new work forms in companies and organisations. 'Pressure from the complex and turbulent competitive environment of the information economy has led to the emergence of new work designs' (Maruping & Agarwal, 2004, p. 975). In order to cope with the new and fast-paced business environment, virtual teams have become an important element of many companies and organisations (Jarvenpaa & Ives, 1994; Hertel et al., 2005), and have therefore captured the imagination of academics and practitioners around the globe (Baker, 2002; Kirkman et al., 2004; Maruping & Agarwal, 2004). The research area is inter-disciplinary; references can be found in social sciences, communication, organisational behaviour, information systems, computer supported teams, distance learning, business administration, and management.

In recent years, more and more virtual teams have emerged in IT companies around the globe. By virtue of the increasing cost pressure in this industry, a steadily rising number of employees working in areas without direct customer contact such as call centres or after-sales support are placed in so-called low-wage[1] countries (e.g. India, Slovakia, Czech Republic). Moreover, virtual teams enable companies to pool talents and experts throughout the world (Furst et al., 2004). As a result, these effects of globalisation lead to an environment in which managers and those who directly report to them are physically separated. However, '... there is growing evidence that virtual teams fail more often than they succeed' (Furst et al., 2004, p.

---

[1] In the literature, the terms low-wage and low-cost are often used interchangeably.

1

6). In many cases, team managers are not sufficiently, or not at all prepared for their leadership role in a virtual team environment (Hertel et al., 2005). The European management of one of the world's largest computer maker XYZ Inc[2], for instance, was not prepared for this change. Most of today's managers gained their management experience with local team members, but now find themselves in a virtual team situation – without having studied the theoretical background or having previous practical experience. In XYZ Europe's marketing department, the change from local to virtual team management was just implemented - virtually overnight - in February 2003, without prior training or preparation for staff or managers. Since then, no time or effort has been invested in understanding virtual team management better. At XYZ Europe, some results of this fast and harsh change from local to virtual personnel management became rapidly visible. These include employees and managers complaining of lack of control[3], missing team spirit, more complicated team leadership due to the prevalent absence of non-verbal communication, proliferation of phone conferences or full email inboxes, all of this resulting in demotivated staff, managerial ineffectiveness, and finally poor results. As a result, XYZ Europe noticed a higher personnel fluctuation and falling employee satisfaction. This was revealed in the results of the internal and anonymous employee survey that takes place twice a year. One area of the survey deals with satisfaction, e.g. 'Do you consider staying at least 18 more months at XYZ?' or 'Would you recommend XYZ as an employer to friends?' Afterwards, each manager is encouraged to discuss the team-related results of the survey and to take measures in order to improve the highlighted problems. This real-world managerial problem became one of the top priorities[4] of XYZ's CEO for 2005. Hence, this DBA project 'Managing Virtual Teams: A Case Study at XYZ Europe' addresses

---

[2] Headquarter in the USA
[3] Due to the fact that the team manager and team members are geographically dispersed.
[4] The first survey revealed that more than fifty percent of the employees are overall not happy or satisfied with their job situation and are therefore looking for alternatives, also outside of XYZ. Consequently, this managerial problem became a top priority.

this challenge and attempts to bridge the gap between theory and practice, between the academic and practical world.

The central research question is:

What makes for the successful management of a virtual team?

Since my research is also intended to improve the current manner of managing virtual teams at XYZ Europe, the following preliminary question needs to be answered first:

How does virtual team management at XYZ Europe currently work?

The findings related to the preliminary question reveal and describe how virtual teams are currently managed in XYZ Europe's real-world environment. The research design is structured in a way to address both questions.

Research Gap and Rationale for this Research

On the one hand, numerous articles written by practitioners are interesting and promising (Kirkman et al., 2004, p. 175), but most of them lack theoretical and academic thoroughness or are too anecdotal in nature. On the other hand, empirical studies meeting academic requirements (Jarvenpaa et al., 1998; Jarvenpaa & Leidner, 1999; Roebuck et al., 2004) mostly

used students performing artificial tasks with unrealistic time limits. To understand what is required for virtual teams, studies examining ongoing virtual work teams performing meaningful, complex tasks in business organizations are now needed (Kirkman et al., 2004, p. 175).

3

In other words, the theoretical assumptions gained from experimental settings need to be examined against real-life conditions (Hertel et al., 2005). Even though virtual teams are becoming increasingly important in various fields, 'little is known about the management of virtual teams and the human resources' (Hertel et al., 2005, p. 89). My DBA project is intended to make a contribution in filling this gap in the existing literature by conducting research in XYZ Europe's marketing department. More precisely, this dissertation attempts to apply as well as challenge the existing knowledge and findings about virtual teams. The research framework is embedded in this particular real-world context for two reasons:

a) to apply and test current theories as well as develop them further

b) to solve a real-world problem at an international IT company

Depending on the findings of the study, this dissertation may or may not support the existing theory and models in the light of XYZ Europe. In addition, this applied research project is expected to solve, or at least improve, a real-world managerial problem bridging theory and practice. The theory and practical knowledge generated from this study will, hopefully, be an original contribution to the body of knowledge in the emerging field of virtual team management in international companies in Europe.

Theoretical and Practical Aims

From a theoretical point of view, this work attempts to contribute to the existing literature in three ways. First, the latest models of virtual team management (Furst et al., 2004; Kerber & Buono, 2004; Maruping & Agarwal, 2004) are applied and examined in the real-world environment of XYZ Europe. Second, in the light of my research findings, it may prove possible to refine current models, or even to develop a new model. Finally, it fills a gap in the literature mentioned above.

The practical component of my project consists of two parts. Its first objective is to investigate the current mode of virtual team management at XYZ Europe in order to understand its key elements and processes better. Using these findings, the second objective is to create an easy-to-use, practical model or set of recommendations, directed towards helping acting managers at XYZ or other companies to lead and organise virtual teams more efficiently through a better understanding of the key success factors and virtual team members' needs.

Boundaries and Limitations

As my research was conducted in XYZ Europe, the findings are therefore not necessarily applicable to other geographic regions or cultural settings. Furthermore, the sample size of this study is small and consequently does not claim to have statistical relevance. Following the paradigm of this project (see Chapter 3), the purpose was to capture a rich and broad understanding of virtual team management, to comprehend the lived experiences of the research objects (interviewees), and finally to provide managerial recommendations for practitioners.

Chapter 2: Literature Review

The only thing I know is that I do not know anything.

Socrates, 470 - 399 B.C.

Introduction

Virtual teams represent an emerging work form and have attracted attention both in theory and practice (Maruping & Agarwal, 2004). As the research spectrum of virtual teams is interdisciplinary, articles, books and other references in areas like business administration, management, team building, distance learning, computer mediated communication, organisational behaviour, and social sciences in general, are considered. Furthermore, since the overall aim of this applied research is to improve the understanding of both the nature of virtual teams in general (theory), and of the challenge of managing virtual teams in European IT companies (practice), this chapter will review the literature relevant to virtual team management in international business environments.

Content and Structure

Since virtual teams are an emerging field in theory, there is a variety of different views and definitions of virtual teams. These are considered and discussed, resulting in a definition suitable for this research project. In addition, characteristics of virtual teams, as well as similarities and differences compared to non-virtual teams, are investigated. Moreover, existing virtual team models are studied and examined for their applicability in practice. Furthermore, two key components of virtual team management, communication and trust, are examined. Even though the research is conducted in an IT company in Europe, this chapter reviews the literature found in other continents in order to provide a broader context for my particular topic.

Current Definitions of Virtual Teams

The existing literature heavily uses the prefix *virtual*: virtual corporation (Davidow & Malone, 1993), virtual teams (Lipnack & Stamps, 1997), virtual task (Mowshowitz, 1999), virtual alliance (Strader et al., 1998), virtual collaboration, virtual organisations (Drucker, 1988; DeSanctis & Jackson, 1994; Lipnack & Stamps, 1997), or virtual project teams. All these terms could be summarised as a kind of virtual *form* (Palmer & Speier, 1997). Before talking about virtual teams, however, it is important to define the expression team itself. What is a non-virtual, that is, a traditional team or collocated[5] team? One of the most cited and widely accepted definition comes from Katzenbach and Smith (1993) in their book *Wisdom of Teams*:

> *A team is a small number of people with complementary skills who are committed to a common purpose, performance goals, and approach for which they are mutually accountable (p. 45).*

How do traditional teams differ from virtual teams? For Grosse (2002), a team becomes virtual if it conducts its work almost entirely through electronic technology. Bell and Kozlowski (2002) define the difference between traditional and virtual teams as follows: 'it is the absence of this proximal, face-to-face interaction between members of virtual teams that makes them virtual' (p. 22). Other authors further define by adding that virtual team members are geographically and organisationally dispersed, rarely meet face-to-face, and rely heavily on technology for task-related communication (Cascio, 2000; Joy-Matthews & Gladstone, 2000). Similarly, Townsend and DeMarie (1998) define virtual teams as

---

[5] Team members working in the same office (not geographically dispersed).

groups of geographically and/or organizationally dispersed co-workers that
are assembled using a combination of telecommunications and information
technologies to accomplish an organizational task (p. 18)

that rarely or even never meet face-to-face. In the most extreme version, team
members have different native languages, remain on different continents in different
countries, interact primarily through computer mediated communication (CMC),
communicate mostly in English, and rarely or even never see or even speak to one
another (Knoll & Jarvenpaa, 1995). Finally, Gibson and Cohen (2003) combine and
refine the above mentioned definitions and consider a team as virtual team if it has
three specific attributes:

- *It is a functioning team - a collection of individuals who are interdependent in*
  their tasks, share responsibility for outcomes, see themselves and are viewed
  by others as an intact social unit embedded in one or more social systems,
  and collectively manage their relationships across organizational boundaries
  (Alderfer, 1977; Hackman, 1987)
- *The members of the team are geographically dispersed*
- *The team relies on technology-mediated communications[6] rather than face-*
  to-face interaction to accomplish their tasks (p. 4)

In addition, Gibson and Cohen (2003) not only discuss what they think a virtual
team is, but also what it is not:

A virtual team is not the same thing as a cross-functional team, a multi-
organizational team, or a multicultural team. This is because it is possible for

---

[6]The terms computer mediated communication (CMC), technology mediated communication (TMC), and
electronically mediated communication (EMC) seem to be applied interchangeably throughout the
literature. Some authors even used the various terms on the same page. For this dissertation, only
electronically mediated communications (EMC) will be used from now on.

a team to be collocated and comprise members from different functions,
organizations, and cultures (p. 5).

Gould (2002) offers a fanciful and easily understandable alternative to define virtual teams, namely a mathematical analogy, an equation:

virtual teams = teams + communication links + groupware[7]

Adding the people management dimension, Hertel et al. (2005) make a distinction between virtual groups and virtual teams:

Virtual groups exist when several teleworkers are combined and each
member reports to the same manager. In contrast, a virtual team exists when
the members of a virtual group interact with each other in order to
accomplish common goals (p. 71).

This distinction seems to me hard to sustain. I argue that not only groups, but also teams can have a manager. I see no reason why a group or virtual group must have a manager, while a team or a virtual team cannot. In order to accomplish a common goal, members of a team may also need a manager steering the team in the right direction. XYZ's virtual teams under study in this research all have common goals and have a manager (team leader) as well.

While most researchers' definitions are similar or close to the ones cited above, a few authors mention neither technology nor geographical dispersion and see virtual organisations more from a process perspective. Hale and Whitlaw (1997) consider a virtual organisation as one that continually evolves, redefines, and reinvents itself for practical business purposes. This view is supported by Katzy (1998),

---

[7] http://www.seanet.com/~daveg/vrteams.htm last viewed March 15th, 2006

Mowshowitz (1997) as well as Venkatraman and Henderson (1998). However, the latest literature (2003 - 2006) shows that the process approach has disappeared.

Since a unique and widely accepted naming convention for virtual forms does not exist, readers of articles and books easily get confused as to the meaning and differentiation of expressions like virtual team, virtual organisation, virtual project team, or virtual group work. Depending on the author, such expressions are sometimes meant to be interchangeable (i.e. synonyms) and sometimes clearly not. In order to prevent confusion, every research project should contain a distinct definition that suits its own needs and purposes. Obviously, anyone else could use an entirely different stipulative definition. For reasons of simplicity, I will exclusively use the term "virtual team" throughout the entire paper. Prior to presenting a definition appropriate to my own project, the characteristics, as well as different types of virtual teams, need to be examined further.

Summary of Characteristics of Virtual Teams

Comparing the various definitions in the literature, the following characteristics of virtual teams that need to be investigated more closely can be filtered out (Table 1).

Table 1: Overview of Characteristics of Virtual and Collocated Team

(Gibson & Cohen, 2003)[8]

Characteristic	Description
Phone or Electronically Mediated Communication	- Telephone, mobile phone (incl. short message system SMS), telefax, phone and/or video conferencing, email, instant messaging (also called chat), electronic white board, groupware (e.g. Lotus Notes), knowledge management system
Geographical Dispersion	- Different offices, buildings, cities, states, countries, continents
Language	- All the same mother tongue (native language, first language) - Different mother tongues but using a common team language (e.g. English) agreed on from the beginning - Different mother tongues, no defined team language (translations needed)
Culture / Religion	- All the same culture/religion - Different cultures/religions
Face-to-Face Communication	- Daily, weekly, monthly, quarterly, yearly, undefined, never
Processes / Rules	- Not defined - Loosely defined - Partially defined - Clearly and strictly defined
Mission	- Not defined - Defined tasks, shared outcome, interdependent members
Time Zone	- All in the same time zone - Some in different time zones - All in different time zones
Duration of Mission	- Short-term, mid-term, long-term, permanent

When comparing various journal articles or research projects, attention needs to be paid to make sure that virtual teams having similar characteristics are compared. XYZ Europe's virtual teams studied in this dissertation all use English as a common language, are geographically dispersed all over Europe, meet face-to-face usually twice a year, have various cultural backgrounds (mainly USA and Europe), work in

---

[8] These characteristics were found in various references cited at the end of this paper, but mainly in Gibson and Cohen (2003).

two time zones (GMT[9] and GMT + 1), use phone as well as electronically mediated communication, and have a common mission (quarterly targets).

Degree of Virtualization

Virtuality can be seen as a continuum (Gibson & Cohen, 2003, p. 5), ranging from slightly virtual to entirely virtual. For example: the more electronically mediated communication (EMC) is used and the more the team members are geographically dispersed, the higher the degree of virtuality. Hertel et al. (2005) also support this view:

> *Instead of trying to draw a clear line between virtual and non-virtual teams, it might be more fruitful to consider the relative "virtuality" of a team (p. 71).*

How could virtuality be measured? Although it is not important for my approach, it might in principle be done by reference to:

- Intensity of use of EMC (Gibson & Cohen, 2003)
- Relation of face-to-face to non-face-to-face communication (Hertel et al., 2005)
- The number of working sites (Kirkman et al., 2004)
- The distance between the members (Hertel et al., 2005)
- The number of different cultures or languages within a virtual team (own measure)

In addition, the degree of virtuality can also be considered from another point of view. Most members of virtual teams not only belong to a virtual community, but are in most cases embedded in a local structure as well. As a result, they belong to two communities: the virtual team and the local team, illustrated in Figure 1:

---

[9] Greenwich Mean Time (London, UK)

12

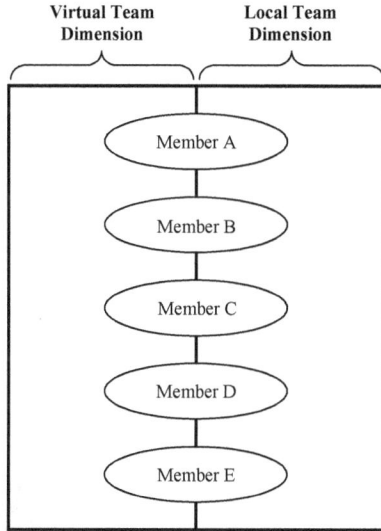

Figure 1: Dual-Membership of Virtual Team Members (developed by the author)

This is also the case at XYZ Europe. Every member of the European virtual marketing team is also part of the local, national XYZ business unit (usually organised country by country[10]). The challenge is obvious: which is the member's primary team and which is the secondary team in terms of questions of priority, workload, or time allocation? Are these team members more local or more virtual? While Figure 1 shows a theoretical case in which all members work 50% in a virtual and 50% in a local team, Figure 2 represents a probably more realistic case, illustrating that local office activities (Wasson, 2004) may vary from member to member or country to country. Example: Virtual team member A may spend more time for the virtual team and less for the local team, while virtual team member B may work more for local activities.

---

[10] Examples: XYZ France SA, XYZ Germany GmbH, or XYZ Switzerland SA

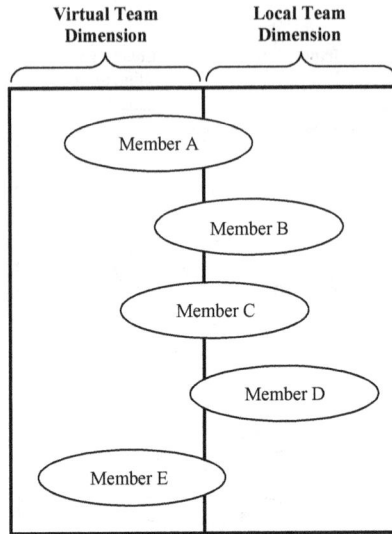

Figure 2: More Realistic Dual-Membership of Virtual Team Members
(developed by the author)

As a result, it can be argued that members A and E have a higher degree of virtuality than members B, C, or D.

Being simultaneously part of a virtual as well as a local team may be advantageous, because every virtual team member then also has regular social face-to-face interactions locally. The risk of feeling isolated (Hertel et al., 2005) is therefore decreased. On the other hand, belonging to two teams increases complexity significantly. First of all, dual-team members usually report to two managers. Hence, they have to cope with demands from both managers and need to strike a balance between both teams' needs. Second, time management becomes more complicated. It may happen that a member should attend a local meeting, and at the same time participate in a conference call with virtual team members. Finally, team managers have to be aware of the fact that some of their subordinates also belong to other teams. Consequently, they have to plan and adjust the team members' workload with the second managers, which increases both the team members' and the team managers' daily workload. As a result, it can be argued that being a member of a virtual team and of a local team demands a great deal of coordination for all involved. This view is widely supported in the literature (Gibson & Cohen, 2003; Furst et al., 2004; Kerber & Buono, 2004; Hertel et al., 2005). Moreover, there appears to be a similarity between virtual teams and matrix organisations with regard to the dual-membership of the team members (Cackowski, 2000; Kuprenas, 2003; Sy & Côté, 2004; Sy & D'Annunzio, 2005). However, it was beyond the scope of this study to investigate this thoroughly.

Further advantages and disadvantages of virtual teams will be discussed in a later chapter.

Types and Illustrations of Virtual Teams

Virtual teams occur not only in high-technology companies, but can nowadays be found in almost any kind of industry or business, such as e-learning, telemedicine, after-sales support for consumer products, call centres, as well as for non-economic organisations (Finholt, 2002; Furst et al., 2004; Kirkman et al., 2004).

Palmer and Speier (1997) tried as pioneering first researchers to establish order in the confusing naming situation of the various virtual forms. Based on their survey of 55 participating organisations, their scheme (Table 2) provides a neat comparison of their four types of virtual forms *virtual team, virtual project, temporary virtual organisation,* and *permanent virtual organisation.*

Table 2: Comparison of Virtual Form Types on Multiple
Dimensions[11]

	virtual team	virtual project	temporary virtual organisation	permanent vo
range of involvement	internal to an organisational function or department unit	across functions and organisations	across organisations	across organisations
membership	small, local	intermediate	typically large	smaller, but scaleable
mission	teams on specific, ongoing tasks	multiple organisational representatives working on spesific projects	multiple functions responding to a market opportunity	all functions and full functionality as a working organisation
length of project	membership varies, but form is permanent	temporary	temporary	permanent
uses of IT	connectivity, sharing embedded knowledge (e-mail, groupware)	repository of shared data (databases, groupware)	shared infrastructutre (groupware, WANs, remote computing)	channel for marketing and distribution, replacing physical infrastructure (web, intra)

Regarding use of terms, however, Palmer and Speier are not always consistent. On one occasion, they use 'virtual model' as an umbrella term, then 'virtual organisation', and later 'virtual form'. A naming convention would have made the article easier to read and the table more applicable for practice and further research. For reasons of simplicity, I will not use their distinctions *virtual team, virtual project, temporary virtual organisation,* and *permanent virtual organisation* in this paper in order to describe and distinguish various virtual teams. Their table, however, was a good starting point for research. For this project, something more practical and suitable is required.

Increasing the terminological confusion, Duarte and Snyder (2001) mention neither virtual organisation nor the term *virtual*, but distinguish seven types of what are in

---

[11] http://virtualni-organizace.aktualne.cz/virtual_organizations.htm last viewed March 15th, 2006

effect virtual teams classified according to the task and the environment in which the team is used (Table 3).

Table 3: The Seven Types of Virtual Teams by Duarte and Snyder (2001, p. 10)

Type of Team	Description
1. Project or Product Development	Team has fluid membership, clear boundaries, a defined customer, and a clear mission. Longer-term team task is non-routine. Team has decision-making authority.
2. Network	Team membership is diffuse and fluid, members come and go as needed. Team lacks clear boundaries and organisation.
3. Parallel	Team has clear boundaries and distinct membership. Team works in short-term to develop recommendations for an improvement in a process or system.
4. Work or Production	Team has distinct membership and clear boundaries. Members perform regular and ongoing work, usually in one functional area.
5. Service	Team has distinct membership and supports ongoing customers. High network activity.
6. Management	Team has distinct membership and works on a regular basis to lead corporate activities.
7. Action	Team deals with immediate action, usually in an emergency situation. Membership may be fluid or distinct.

However, this approach also seems to be too complex and not applicable for practically oriented applied research. First of all, a graphic overview is missing. In an unsettled real-world environment, graphs, diagrams, or any other kind of graphic illustrations are preferable to a simple text or table, as they allow the reader to gain an understanding much faster. Secondly, neither Table 2 nor Table 3 takes into account that in today's rapidly changing work environments, the structures of organisations as well as work forms in general need to be revised and adapted on a regular basis (Filos, 2006). For this applied research, the ideal illustration of a virtual team should show:

- where virtual teams derived from (the traditional hierarchical organisational structure)
- that other, specific skills are needed to able to cope with the new environment
- the geographical dispersion
- the multi-cultural dimension

while also leaving room for future adaptations. Filos' recent article (2006, p. 9) introduced a very interesting and promising illustration of virtual teams taking these criteria into consideration (Figure 3):

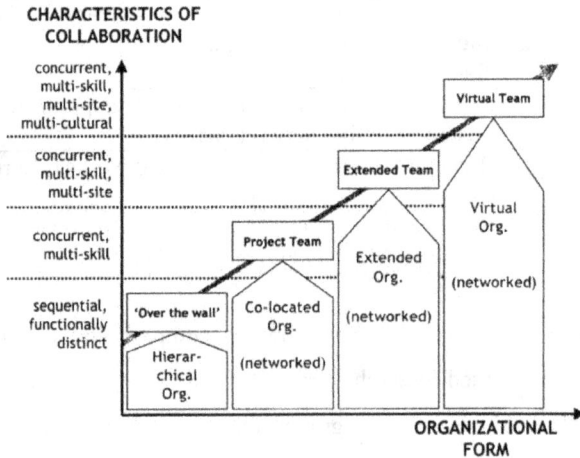

Figure 3: The Evolution of Collaborative Work and the Impact on Organisational Forms

In order to clarify and simplify the use of terms in this dissertation, only the term *virtual team* based on both Filos' (2006) illustration as well as Gibson and Cohen's (2003) definition will be used from now on. Different types of virtual teams will be distinguished using the characteristics discussed in previous paragraphs (see Table 1).

Advantages and Drawbacks of Virtual Teams

It is widely accepted that a high degree of virtuality adds a complexity to the team that needs to be taken into consideration (Gibson & Cohen, 2003; Furst et al., 2004; Kerber & Buono, 2004; Kirkman et al., 2004). So, what are the advantages of virtual teams? What can virtual teams do better than collocated ones, and what are the challenges and disadvantages that the increased complexity causes? The advantages and disadvantages can be categorised into three groups: personal level, organisational level, and societal level (Hertel et al., 2005).

Advantages of Virtual Teams

At the Personal Level

Virtual team members may experience a higher personal job satisfaction thanks to

- a higher work flexibility (less direct supervision and increased freedom to plan daily tasks)
- higher responsibilities (e.g. responsible for an international instead of just a local project, or leading several independent projects)
- the possibility of experiencing new cultures and learning new languages while dealing with people from other countries
- the possibility of applying previously studied language skills
- occasional travel for important training or project kick-off meetings (business travel can be combined with private interests, e.g. staying the weekend in another city)

and can therefore foster the employee's motivation (Gibson & Cohen, 2003; Hertel et al., 2005; Filos, 2006).

At the Organisational Level

Virtual teams significantly increase knowledge sharing (Gibson & Cohen, 2003; Furst et al., 2004) and bring talents from around the globe - anytime and everywhere - together (Kerber & Buono, 2004) that would not be able to work jointly for cost and time reasons. For example: very valuable employees who are not willing, or not in a position, to relocate can be retained, so vital knowledge does not get lost. In addition, best practices from all over the world can be shared reducing the number of errors by using other employees' prior experiences. Moreover, employees can be hired in low-wage regions in order to significantly decrease the companies operating expenses (e.g. call centres for presales or customer care services). Furthermore, virtual teams considerably reduce costs of travelling, as well as decrease the amount of unproductive time, such as the actual travel time, and delayed or even cancelled flights (Hertel et al., 2005). From an organisational point of view, Grenier and Metes (1995) consider virtual teams to be the key success factor for the 21st century.

At the Societal Level

Virtual teams offer new opportunities for people with low mobility, family care duties, or even disabilities. Thanks to higher work flexibility, they can first take their kids to school or a medical appointment before going to work. Where companies offer the possibility of home-office[12], the work productivity of external sales representatives can raise considerably, because home-office allows them to do the paper work at home, thus no time loss driving to the office before visiting the customers. Finally, it results in an overall lower environmental pollution due to reduced commuting traffic and air pollution (Hertel et al., 2005).

---

[12] Working from home using a laptop which is connected to the company's private network via internet.

20

Drawbacks of Virtual Teams

At the Personal Level

Having less face-to-face interaction with team members may cause a feeling of isolation and detachment depending on the degree of virtuality (Kirkman et al., 2002; Hertel et al., 2005; Filos, 2006). In addition, the dual-membership of most virtual team members[13] increases the chances of misunderstandings, and therefore result in more numerous conflict escalations. This is partially related to the fact that belonging to two teams increases work complexity in terms of priority setting, workload balance, and individual time management. Also, each member has to deal with more stakeholders, further complicating work and communication. Moreover, from a technology point of view, more communication tools like phone, email, instant messaging[14], or video conferencing are available and are used more often. Finally, working with a person one has never met or seen before (Handy, 1995) adds additional challenges in terms of trust levels and building trust within virtual teams (Jarvenpaa et al., 1998; Jarvenpaa & Leidner, 1999; Kirkman et al., 2002; Gibson & Cohen, 2003; Filos, 2006).

At the Organisational Level

Collocated and virtual teams face similar challenges, but time, language, distance and limited face-to-face communication compound them (Burtha & Connaughton, 2004; Kerber & Buono, 2004). The reduced, or total absence of face-to-face communication in particular, can potentially lead to misunderstandings and conflicts, since the non-verbal cues like smiles, voice levels, or raised eyebrows are mostly missing or restricted (Wilson, 2003). From a managerial point of view, virtual teams increase the complexity of team management due to lack of control caused by the geographical dispersion of the team members. For daily life, it simply means that team managers do not see their subordinates most of the time (Pauleen,

---

[13] Belonging to a virtual as well to a local team at the same time.
[14] Instant messaging (IM) is a virtual chat room where text messages can be easily and rapidly exchanged.

21

2003; Hertel et al., 2005). Another managerial challenge is building and maintaining trust and relationships at a distance (Pauleen, 2003). In addition, cultural differences such as punctuality, working speed, quality perception, conflict management, or priority setting (Schermerhorn et al., 2000), as well as accessing and leveraging the immense sources of knowledge (Roebuck et al., 2004; Filos, 2006), call for new skills for virtual team members and managers. Filos (2006) argues that

> *as virtual teams are made up of individuals with human needs for belonging, communicating, and togetherness, a radically new approach of virtual team management is needed (p. 10).*

Comprehensive training may be one possibility to fill this gap. Moreover, the emergence of the term *virtual team experience*[15] points to this issue. Furthermore, a virtual environment causes higher technology and infrastructure costs, like numerous and long phone calls or even phone conferences, higher network traffic, more applications[16], and therefore higher licensing fees. Finally, regular training is required to make sure the employees can profit from all of the investments. From a short-term perspective, training also adds cost, and temporarily reduces the employee's productivity because during training, they can not do their regular work. Eventually, costs for trainers as well as for training facilities add up.

Trust in Virtual Teams

Trust seems to be of major importance in virtual teams (Handy, 1995; Jarvenpaa et al., 1998; Jarvenpaa & Leidner, 1999; Gibson & Cohen, 2003; Pauleen, 2003; Alge et al., 2004; Brown et al., 2004; Kirkman et al., 2004; Hertel et al., 2005; Dani et al., 2006; Filos, 2006) and is mentioned by almost everyone who writes on the topic.

---

[15] 12 out of 18 interviewees agreed that virtual team experience is a particular skill that should even be mentioned in a C.V.
[16] Hardware and software for instant messaging (IM), video-conferencing, netmeeting or other sort of groupware.

O'Hara-Devereaux and Johansen (1994) argue that 'Trust is the glue of the global workspace' (p. 243). In addition, communication, especially the replacement for face-to-face communication, plays an important role. Moreover, a new style of leadership is needed (Pauleen, 2003) to build and maintain trust through virtual communication; remote control comes into play (Alge et al., 2004).

Trust and Initial Trust

Trust is variously understood in the literature (Hosmer, 1995). However, there is no globally accepted and widely used scholarly definition of trust. For this dissertation, the following definition is used

> *[Trust] is the willingness of a party to be vulnerable to the actions of another party based on the expectation that the other party will perform a particular action important to the trustor, irrespective of the ability to monitor or control that other party (Mayer et al., 1995, p. 712).*

It includes elements relevant for this research dealing with people working in a team environment: willingness, expectations of performance, monitoring and controlling. The definition of Mayer et al., however, incorporates only the relationship of one party with a second party. As a virtual team mostly consists of more than two people, I would like to add one more element to the definition of Mayer et al.: collective trust. According to Gibson and Cohen (2003), collective trust is a crucial element in dealing with virtual teams. The authors define collective trust as

> *a shared psychological state in a team that is characterized by an acceptance of vulnerability based on expectations of intentions or behaviours of others within the team (p. 59).*

In a team with a high level of collective trust, each member believes that other members will make every effort to meet agreed expectations, be open and honest in any type of communication, and will not take advantage of other members (Cummings & Bromiley, 1996). Adding the term collective trust emphasises the fact that in conventional as well as virtual teams, trust is not only something between two members, but represents a 1-to-many relationship.

Focusing now on virtual teams, the cultural dimension also needs to be taken into account. Due to the nature of virtual teams, people from diverse countries, having different cultural backgrounds, work together. Culture can be seen as a shared understanding and sense making, sets of unofficial rules, general behaviours, and non-stated beliefs of a cultural entity (Schein, 1993). The cultural dimension can be categorised into three levels (Gibson & Cohen, 2003):

- National level (e.g. Dutch culture compared to Italian culture)
- Organisational or company-related level (e.g. XYZ's company culture compared to BMW's company culture)
- Functional level (e.g. sales culture compared to engineering culture)

The cultural dimension is important because culture affects the hidden and unspoken expectations of the virtual team members. Different expectations can lead to misunderstandings, can therefore influence the individual's as well as the team's performance, and are consequently, according to the chosen definition, linked to trust. This understanding is important, as it further divides the term trust into initial trust and experienced trust (McKnight et al., 1998).

It is commonly argued that trust can be built over time (Jarvenpaa & Leidner, 1999; Kirkman et al., 2002; Brown et al., 2004; Maruping & Agarwal, 2004). If trust can be built over time, what existed before the trust-building process started? McKnight et al. (1998) define it as initial trust. As soon as a person interacts with another person for the very first time (be it face-to-face, on the phone, via email or using any other form of communication), one automatically and unconsciously allocates a certain level of trust towards the other person. Initial trust levels vary significantly, depending on previous experiences or cultural background. It can be argued that from a managerial point of view, initial trust is a given, since it is something personal and linked to the individual's previous life experiences before becoming a member of the team. To a certain extent, the initial trust level might be affected by making team members aware of it through discussion or training. However, from a team development perspective, it seems to be more important to know how to build and strengthen trust over time, irrespective of initial trust levels of team members in the beginning.

Building Trust

In order to answer the question of whether a team without any prior working experience, and no initial face-to-face meeting, can successfully work together and build trust, Handy (1995) named seven cardinal principles that need to be considered:

1. Trust is not blind
2. Trust needs boundaries
3. Trust demands learning
4. Trust is tough
5. Trust needs bonding
6. Trust needs touch
7. Trust requires leaders

Especially principle 6, "Trust needs touch", became a focal point for virtual team researchers. Jarvenpaa and Leidner (1999) argue that in virtual teams, trust requires a great deal of face-to-face interaction, if possible even constantly. However, this is somehow contradictory, since a virtual team in its nature in fact eliminates or at least reduces face-to-face communication. Building trust between team members who seldom, or even never, see each other seems to be a major challenge for virtual teams. According to Gibson and Cohen (2003), 'communication processes are the key underlying mechanisms for establishing trust' (p. 69). Based on a study at Sabre Inc, Kirkmann et al. (2002) assume that virtual team members have a notably higher level of trust after spending time together sharing meals, discussing private interests, or socialising after business hours. It can be argued that having the possibility of meeting face-to-face in the beginning of a virtual team's life cycle has a positive effect on people's mutual trust levels. Moreover, the positive impact of an early face-to-face meeting can be amplified by planning specific social activities such as:

- Social chat: exchanging personal information (e.g. family or former jobs)
- Exchanging pictures
- Distributing a personal information sheet to other team members prior to the first face-to-face meeting

This is supported by a series of studies on the effects of early social activities on trust, conducted by Zheng et al. (2002). The researchers demonstrated that early social interactions (even if carried out online) may significantly increase team members' mutual trust. Their view corresponds well with other studies (Jarvenpaa & Leidner, 1999; Kirkman et al., 2002). Therefore, it seems that virtual teams might build trust if team members get engaged in some form of social interaction in the very beginning of the team's life.

What needs to be done after the initial trust-building activities in order to continuously build trust? Or what can be undertaken if an initial trust-building activity is not possible at all? Some authors suggest regular and constructive feedback as one form of building trust over time, be it face-to-face, on the phone, or via EMC (Gibson & Cohen, 2003; Maruping & Agarwal, 2004). Furthermore, Gibson and Cohen (2003) suggest regular virtual team meetings, to create a sort of team 'togetherness': For team managers, they recommend a regular call with every team member (1-to-1 communication) to discuss the individual's personal needs as well as a regular team call with the entire team (many-to-many communication) addressing topics related and relevant to the team. However, I argue that this only works successfully if team members actually do care and do want these calls; simply imposing instructions without acceptance of the team might not work. In addition, Hertel et al. (2005) claim that non-job-related communication correlates positively with team productivity, as well as team members' satisfaction, and finally builds trust. Their view is supported by other studies (Zheng et al., 2002; Hertel et al., 2004). For that reason, it can be argued that positive causal relations exist between non-job-related communication and mutual trust in virtual teams. Finally, how could trust be measured? While later chapters will discuss various levels of trust (e.g. high, low, or increased trust), trying to quantify trust is beyond the scope of this dissertation. Further research may address this.

High-Trust and Low-Trust Teams

How does a team with a high level of trust differ from one with a low level of trust? By observing a virtual team and its behaviour, how can one rapidly identify the team's level of trust? A study conducted by Jarvenpaa et al. (1998) used a pattern-matching approach 'to infer behaviours and strategies common to the high-trust teams but less common to, or nonexistent in, the low-trust teams' (p. 52). Their findings are summarised in Table 4.

Table 4: Strategies between High- and Low-Trust Teams by Jarvenpaa et al. (1998)

Strategy or Behaviour	High-Trust Teams	Low-Trust Teams
Style of Action	Proactive	Reactive
Team Spirit	Optimistic	Pessimistic
Team Leadership	Dynamic, Adaptive	Static
Pattern of Interaction	Regular, Frequent	Infrequent
Nature of Feedback	Predictable	Unpredictable

Interpersonal Trust versus Task-Based Trust

Kirkman et al. (2002) question the conventional thinking that building trust absolutely requires face-to-face communication or touch, and argue that in order to build trust in a virtual team, face-to-face communication is not a mandatory prerequisite. Their study revealed that trust can also be built virtually; the question is however what type of trust is developed. Drawing on Mayer (1995), the authors divide trust into interpersonal trust and task-based trust. While the former is built through face-to-face interactions, the latter occurs if virtual team members without prior face-to-face interactions keep commitments, prove to be reliable, cooperative, and helpful, as well as constantly deliver a high quality of work to achieve the commonly defined team goals. The following table summarises the activities building either interpersonal or task-based trust (Kirkman et al., 2002).

Table 5: Overview of Activities Building Interpersonal and Tasked-Based Trust

Building Interpersonal Trust	Building Task-Based Trust
• Sharing meals • Socialising after business hours • Sharing personal information and hobbies • Exchanging pictures • Non-job-related communication	• Keeping team commitments and deadlines • Constantly delivering high quality work • Reliable, helpful, cooperative behaviour

Communication

Using electronically mediated communication (EMC) more often than face-to-face communication (FTF) is one of the defining characteristics of virtual teams (Gibson & Cohen, 2003; Andres, 2006; Brake, 2006). Even though non-virtual and collocated teams can use the same tools of communication, the frequency and the degree virtual teams rely on EMC differs significantly. For example: two members of a local team meeting one another by chance in the cafeteria can quickly discuss a topic and then send a quick confirmation or summary email for filing purposes. In a virtual team, you do not just meet someone by chance: one either has an appointment or has to try to reach the other person by phone or electronically. If the member cannot be reached via phone, sending an email might be an option. In this case, the email content would be much longer and more detailed compared to the summary email.

Phone, voice mail, e-mail, video-conferencing, and instant messaging are powerful tools to share information within virtual teams and allow members to choose between several tools of communication. Compared to face-to-face communication, however, they lack richness. Paralinguistic cues like loudness or hesitations, as well as visual cues, are not transmitted (Gibson & Cohen, 2003). As a result, the likelihood of misunderstandings resulting in conflicts increases (Chawla & Krauss, 1994). Cramton (2001; 2002) comes to the same conclusion, but her research takes a more detailed examination. First, she argues that people tend to assume that the other team members' local situation is similar. Therefore, they take circumstances like infrastructure, equipment, working style, or business hours for granted. As a result, their communication does not include all the necessary information to guarantee that the receiver fully understands the message, which can lead to misunderstandings. Secondly, the findings of her study state that due to the lack of visual and paralinguistic cues, virtual team members have a higher tendency to interpret parts of a message differently. They may overlook some parts of the message that the senders considers as crucial. Thus, the receiver's interpretation may change, and therefore influence the response or subsequent actions. As a result, she concludes that visual and paralinguistic cues also signal importance and increase the receiver's understanding of which parts of the message are more important. This finding leads to the next challenge of virtual team communication Cramton addressed: problems of confirmation. In order to reduce the risk of misunderstanding, the sender of a message unconsciously tries to verify whether the receiver understood the message. A virtual team member may look either for a reaction confirming that the receiver understood and agrees with the message, or for indications of misunderstandings or disagreement. Possible confirmations may be verbal or non-verbal. Table 6, created by the author of this dissertation, illustrates this finding and gives some practical examples.

Table 6: Overview of Verbal and Non-Verbal Elements for Confirmation

	Verbal	Non-Verbal
Signalling understanding or agreement	Statements like • Ok! • Good idea! • I like that! • Sounds good to me!	Reactions like • Nodding • Pleased and unworried facial expression
Signalling misunderstanding or disagreement	Statements like • Hmmm... • Are you sure? • I am not sure! • So...	Reactions like • Shaking of the head • Concerned facial expression

Consequently, it seems evident that messages are understood more accurately and the risk of misunderstanding is significantly lower when paralinguistic and visual cues are available (Chawla & Krauss, 1994; Cramton, 2001, 2002; Gibson & Cohen, 2003). This idea coincides with the media richness theory of Draft and Lengel (1984).

Multitasking in Virtual Teams

A typical and rather frequent form of communication in virtual teams is multitasking. During conference calls, team members can easily have a side conversation (putting the phone on mute), read reports, use instant messaging, or read and write emails when not speaking. Gibson and Cohen (2003) believe that overall, multitasking has a negative impact on virtual team communication and productivity. First, it distracts team members leading to 'additional redundant discussions due to missed or only partially heard discussions' (p. 390). Furthermore, a distracted team member can miss opportunities to give feedback or provide input to the discussion.

On the other hand, Wasson (2004) conducted a field study in an organisation with long-term virtual team experiences and concluded that multitasking 'could enhance employee productivity when properly managed' (p. 47). The author admits that multitasking may have a negative impact on a team's productivity when a team member is not sufficiently skilled at distributing attention, or cannot rapidly distinguish between relevant and irrelevant topics. She argues, however, that overall, the advantages clearly outweigh the disadvantages. Even before virtual teams first appeared, employees raised concerns about the productivity of face-to-face meetings, calling them a 'poor use of their time' (p. 56). In such meetings, not every topic is relevant to every participant, resulting in bored participants and loss of time. Consequently, Wasson (2004) concludes that thanks to the emergence of virtual teams as well as technological progress, multitasking allows participants to spend their time more wisely and more effectively. This is supported by statements made by participants of her research (for more information about the participants of her study see Wasson (2004)) such as:

I am glad we went to virtual meetings because when we were all meeting in a room, it was impossible to get work done in a unproductive meeting (p. 56).

Table 7 summarises the last two sections comparing the characteristics of FTF and EMC.

Table 7: Comparison of Characteristics between FTF and EMC

Characteristics	FTF	EMC
Richness of Information	High	Lower
Transmission of Visual cues	Yes	No
Transmission of Paralinguistic Cues (Loudness, Hesitations)	Yes	No
Confirmation	Easy	Complicated
Likelihood of Multitasking	Low	Higher
Risk of Misunderstandings	Low	Higher

Models of Virtual Teams

What is a model? The Oxford Dictionary of English (Soanes & Stevenson, 2003) defines a model as 'a simplified mathematical description of a system or process, used to assist calculations and predictions'. Linking it to my research project, I regard a model as a tool that serves practitioners, like managers or team members, to more easily understand a complex real-world situation. During the literature review, three models suitable for an applied research on the topic of virtual teams were found.

Stage Models

Tuckman (1965) based his Stage Model of Team Development on research conducted in a local team environment. It is composed of four stages: forming (unbridled optimism), storming (reality shock), norming (refocus and recommitment), and performing. According to the author, building a team starts with forming: team members share relevant information about themselves as well as their work. This takes place in discussions or implicitly via non-verbal clues. During the first stage, the team is expected to build trust and to define clear objectives. Afterward, in the 'storming' stage, the first team conflicts arise due to misunderstandings or differing opinions. In the next stage called 'norming', they resolve their problems and agree on clear team rules and principles. Ultimately, the team reaches the 'performing' stage: They work towards the agreed objectives and support one another whenever possible. Furst et al. (2004, p. 15) applied Tuckman's model in a virtual team environment. The objective of their applied research was to present some guidelines and recommendations for people managing or working in virtual teams. Figure 4 summarises the authors' findings.

Formation	Storming	Norming	Performing
• Realistic virtual project team previews	• Face-to-face team building sessions	• Create customized templates or team charters specifying task requirements	• Ensure departmental and company culture supports virtual team work
• Coaching from experienced team members	• Training on conflict resolution	• Set individual accountabilities, completion dates, and schedules	• Provide sponsor support and resources for team to perform
• Develop a shared understanding and sense of team identity	• Encourage conflicting employees to work together to find common ground	• Establish procedures for information sharing	
• Develop a clear mission	• Shuttle diplomacy and mediation to create compromise solutions	• Distinguish task, social, and contextual information; design procedures appropriate for each	
• Acquire senior manager support		• Assign a team coach with skills for managing virtually	

Figure 4: Managerial Interventions during the Virtual Project Team Life Cycle

34

Tuckman's initial model, adapted for virtual teams by Furst et al. (2004), is easy to understand and provides clear indications for managers on what needs to be done and when. However, it is static[17] and reveals neither connections nor interactions between team members. In addition, it neglects external elements (e.g. cultural differences or the dual-membership of virtual team members) influencing the team.

Hertel et al. (2005) also developed a stage model, but one composed of five stages as shown in Figure 5.

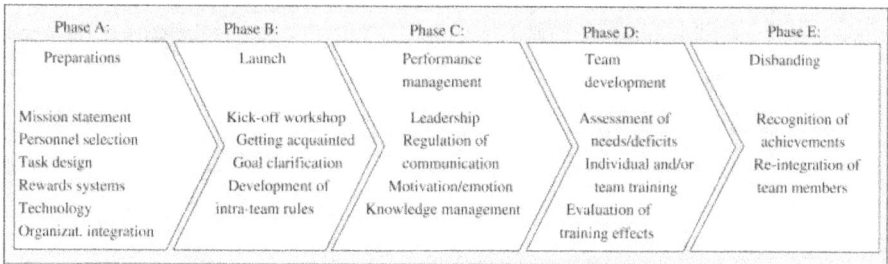

Phase A:	Phase B:	Phase C:	Phase D:	Phase E:
Preparations	Launch	Performance management	Team development	Disbanding
Mission statement	Kick-off workshop	Leadership	Assessment of	Recognition of
Personnel selection	Getting acquainted	Regulation of	needs/deficits	achievements
Task design	Goal clarification	communication	Individual and/or	Re-integration of
Rewards systems	Development of	Motivation/emotion	team training	team members
Technology	intra-team rules	Knowledge management	Evaluation of	
Organizat. integration			training effects	

Figure 5: Key Activities in the Life Cycle of Virtual Team Management (p. 73)

Compared with the four-stage model (Figure 4) which states not only *what* needs to be done (e.g. building the team) but also *how* it can be realised (e.g. through face-to-face meetings), Hertel et al.'s model only states what should be achieved (e.g. team development), but gives no indication on how this could be accomplished. Consequently, it is less relevant to practitioners. In addition, like the first model, it is static too.

---

[17] By static, I mean that a model simply describes something in words, without visualising relationships or actions.

Virtual Team Dynamics Model

The Virtual Team Dynamics Model (Figure 6) developed by Kerber and Buono (2004) goes one step further and takes the dynamic dimension into account. It addresses the relations and interactions amongst team members and does not neglect external elements. Team members are portrayed as circles, the team leader as a triangle. While the chosen forms do not seem to have a specific meaning, putting the leader in the centre and not traditionally on the top of a hierarchical organisational chart[18] is particularly interesting. Does it mean that the team leader is not a decision-maker, but more a team coordinator without having authority or decision power (primus inter pares[19])? The leader's central position may also imply that this position is not fixed but rather temporary (job rotation), a known behaviour from the field of ornithology studying leadership behaviour of migratory birds. However, this is not explicitly mentioned by the authors. Becker (2001) as well as Scott and Einstein (2001) highly suggest job rotation in virtual teams as it provides equal opportunities for all team members to learn, develop, and gain leadership experience; resulting in higher motivation and mutual trust.

---

[18] Also called org-chart or organigram
[19] Latin: first among equals

36

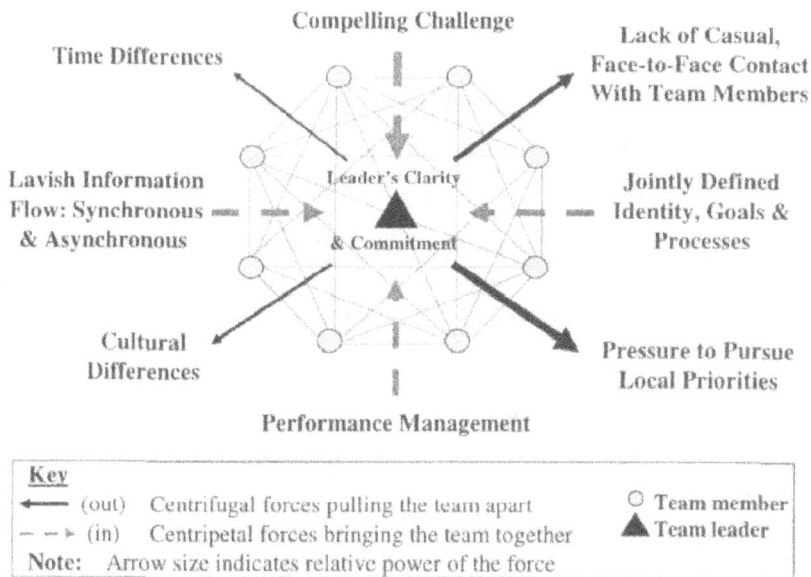

Figure 6: Dynamics in a Global Virtual Team (p. 8)

Furthermore, the fine lines in the model demonstrate all the possible paths of communication between team members, also showing that the entire communication does not necessarily have to go through the team leader (lateral communication). Moreover, the researchers added centrifugal and centripetal forces visualised by arrows, a very valuable part of this graphical illustration of virtual team dynamics. The centrifugal forces (bold lines) present elements with possible negative impacts on the virtual team's cohesion and success. For examples: cultural difference, different time zones, or lack of face-to-face communication, all of which complicate team interactions and processes. The centripetal forces (dashed lines), by contrast, indicate positive, supportive effects like joint team objectives or being motivated by the international dimension of the environment. In addition, the thickness of the arrows also contains relevant information specifying the strength of influence: thin arrows stand for low impact or low weight, whereas thick ones mean strong influence or high weight. However, I find one element of this presentation implausible. The authors consider lavish information flow as supportive and positive. Based on my personal experience in virtual teams, supported by numerous researchers (Shapiro & Varian, 1999; Kirkman et al., 2002; Gibson & Cohen, 2003; Maruping & Agarwal, 2004; Wasson, 2004; Filos, 2006), I hold that in most cases, the contrary is true. A lavish information flow leads to 'overabundant information' (Filos, 2006, p. 11) and uncoordinated communication, causing numerous emails, phone calls, or misunderstandings in general. Herbert Simon's[20] famous citation concisely explains it: 'What information consumes is rather obvious: it consumes the attention of its recipients. Hence, a wealth of information creates a poverty of attention.'[21]

Finally, Kerber and Buono's model correlates to a high degree with the characteristics of virtual teams (see Table 1). Except for the last characteristic (duration of mission), all the others are somehow integrated in the model.

Summary and Consequences for the Research

This chapter analysed and compared characteristics and definitions of virtual teams, with a view to developing a definition suitable for this research project. The advantages and disadvantages of virtual teams from a personal, organisational, and societal point of view were outlined. Moreover, the key topics of trust and communication were discussed. Keeping the practical aim of the research in mind, implications for practice like initial trust, and trust building, as well as the limitations and hidden dangers of EMC, were investigated. Further, one dynamic and two static models of virtual teams were examined and partially revised. The findings were incorporated in the development of the semi-structured interview (see Chapter 3, Data Collection). Finally, reviewing the literature revealed the literature gap discussed in Chapter 1 and thus provided the basis for this applied research project, which is aimed at improving the understanding of both the nature of virtual

---

[20] Herbert Simon, June 15th 1916 - February 9th 2001, researcher and Nobel Prize winner in 1978
[21] http://www.worldofquotes.com/author/Herbert-Simon/1/index.html last viewed March 9th 2006

teams in general (theory), and of the challenge of managing virtual teams in European IT companies (practice).

Chapter 3: Research Methodology and Design

In addition to the description of the research problem in Chapter 1, the current challenges of virtual team management at XYZ Europe can be stated as follows:

- an unclear, hazy situation: lack of a clear problem statement from XYZ's management
- people and teams with different cultural backgrounds and languages working together
- overload of communication and daily interactions (e.g. being swamped by more than 100 emails or several hours of conference calls a day)
- managers' lack of understanding of processes combined with lack of preparation for managing virtual teams

What methodology and methods should be applied to a situation like this? A methodology is generally understood as a strategy of inquiry which starts with the underlying philosophical assumptions and progresses to research design, data collection and analysis (Hussey & Hussey, 1997; Prasad, 1997; Punch, 2000; Silverman, 2000). The research methodology employed therefore has highly significant implications for the way the researcher collects, analyses, and interprets data. In other words, the choice of a research methodology influences the selection of the research methods applied in a study.

Quantitative versus Qualitative Research

While quantitative research is rooted and widely used in natural sciences, qualitative research is often more appropriate for social science researchers concerned with social forms of interaction, with people's lived experiences and everyday behaviour (Silverman, 2000). 'Qualitative research reveals people's values, interpretative schemes, mind maps, belief systems and rules of living so that the respondent's reality can be understood' (Cavana et al., 2001, p. 34). Silverman (2000) also argues that researchers using qualitative research methods have a common conviction that their approach 'can provide a deeper understanding of social phenomena than would be obtained from purely quantitative data' (p. 89). However, quantitative and qualitative research should not be considered as a sharp division, but rather as a continuum (Hussey & Hussey, 1997; Punch, 2000; Silverman, 2000). Moreover, some researchers combine methods from both paradigms and call it triangulation (Ragin & Becker, 1992; Gable, 1994). In most cases, using multiple methods may increase the level of validity and reliability, a common weakness of purely qualitative research (Collis & Hussey, 2003). The authors claim that applying multiple methods correlates positively with validity and reliability if findings and conclusions derived from different methods are similar or even equal.

I hold that a qualitative approach is well positioned and appropriate to address my research questions stated in Chapter 1. My intention is to explore these questions emphasizing 'understanding', which is in particular important for the preliminary research question[22]. Wasson (2004) argues that a qualitative approach allows to discover better what the people 'being studied actually do rather than what they think or say they do in surveys' (p. 50). Therefore, a chiefly qualitative study seems to be more suitable than a quantitative one to comprehend the situation and its dynamics as well as to access and unveil people's tacit knowledge and hidden capabilities. To address the central research question (What makes for the successful management of a virtual team?), I need to capture and examine processes, their meanings and implications, as well as people's concerns and ideas. The latter is especially important from a practical point of view, as virtual team management at XYZ Europe should be improved. I assume that this can be reached better by closely examining people's assertions and behaviour (through observation) rather than assigning mathematical formulas or using intensive and complex statistics.

---

[22] Preliminary research question: How does virtual team management at XYZ Europe currently work?

Positivist, Interpretivist, or Critical Research?

Overall, I am dealing with a largely positivist, universalising, and generalising literature, aiming at providing the foundations for a technology of management. I also wish to provide something that will be of use to the management of virtual teams in general and in the light of XYZ Europe. However, this dissertation intends to approach the existing literature, theories, and models more critically. Since they are universalising, at least in ambition and claims, it will be interesting to see to what extent they say anything useful, explanatory, or suggestive about XYZ Europe. As this study is meant to provide something valuable about virtual teams in general, as well as something for XYZ Europe, I adopt a mixed methodology. The research starts from a positivist ground, then moves to chiefly interpretivist and critical philosophical assumptions for the middle part, and finishes mainly rooted in positivism for the implications for practice. In other words, I am not adopting a methodologically pure approach throughout, but consciously move from one approach (in the field-work and in-house conclusions) to another, more positivist one in terms of the theoretical bearing.

Positivist research aims at discovering universal and predictive laws. Therefore, positivist researchers assume that all people have the same meaning systems, or that meaning systems are insignificant or secondary to something else. On the other hand, interpretivist and constructivist research are based on the belief that reality is socially constructed and that the 'world is largely what people perceive it to be' (Cavana et al., 2001, p. 9). Consequently, researchers following an interpretivist or constructivist paradigm attempt to reveal how people feel and react in certain real-world situations, raising the *understanding* of this particular case or similar ones. While constructivism emphasises *constructing* the reality, interpretivism focuses on *unveiling* the reality. Having the preliminary research question in mind, I chose an interpretative approach because before a situation can be improved (here virtual team management at XYZ Europe), one first needs to comprehend the current situation. Therefore, the reality needs to be investigated.

The central research question, however, calls for another philosophical assumption as it is not only intended to understand a particular context, but to improve it - in my case the virtual team management at XYZ Europe. I believe that critical management research is the appropriate philosophical assumption to address the needs of improvement as it is largely concerned with subverting organisations and current management methods. According to Cavana et al. (2001), critical management research 'is to empower people to create a better world for themselves' (p. 10). In other words, it stimulates change and serves as a catalyst leading to transformation. In addition, the authors hold that people have a great deal of hidden potential and the capability of making progress and transforming themselves. To foster this, myths and circumstances taken for granted need to be revealed. This view is supported by Alvesson and Deetz (2000) proposing a three-step model to conduct critical research (p. 146):

1. **Producing Insight**

   Once the research objects are made aware of situations or elements taken for granted, they become more motivated to make changes in their lives (Cavana et al., 2001, p. 10).

2. **Producing Critique**

   Thanks to the new perception of the situation after step one, the researcher can now question and challenge the traditional views and hence create an environment in which new ideas and suggestions can arise. In this phase, people might also discover unrealised and hidden abilities.

3. Producing Transformative Re-Definition

Finally, the findings may stimulate the research participants to partially transform themselves, rejecting some of the former habits and/or applying the newly gained knowledge.

In addition, Alvesson and Deetz (2000) name two salient concepts in order to build a critical research environment: de-familiarisation and negation (pp. 165-175). The former is supposed to turn 'the well-known into the exotic' (p. 167). When writing or talking to research objects, the well-known should be presented in such a way that is does not sound familiar any more. For example: traditionally, a team consists of several team members and a team manager having official authority and a certain level of power. Turning it into the exotic could mean: What if a team does not have a classic manager any more, but the team members share the managerial tasks and responsibilities in most cases? Starting from this unfamiliar point of view creates a certain distance to current perception (Alvesson & Deetz, 2000, p. 169) and builds the critical research environment necessary to foster change that may lead to improvements. The second concept is intended to work with negations or countertext. The authors assume that 'by negating existing reality… fruitful insights can be achieved' (p. 172), allowing people to see the well-known in a different and meaningful way. Eventually, in some respects but not all, this study will conform to the approach of critical management research. Alvesson and Deetz's (2000) three-step model, as well as the their two proposed concepts de-familiarisation and negation, are incorporated in the research design described below.

Philosophical Assumptions for my Research

Finally, bearing the objectives and needs of both research questions in mind, I apply a mixture of interpretivist and critical research as shown in Figure 7.

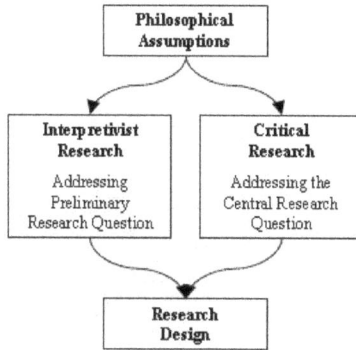

Figure 7: Philosophical Assumption

The structure of the following research design builds upon these assumptions. However, purely interpretative studies make it difficult to generalise and predict behavioural connections in virtual teams. Taking the objective of improving the current manner of managing virtual teams by providing recommendations for acting XYZ managers into consideration, conclusions and recommendations may be strongly coloured by positivism (generalising management theory).

Research Design

The research project is designed as an ethnographic study. This methodology includes observations and interviews (Atkinson & Hammersley, 1994; Prasad, 1997) and is therefore 'particularly suited to examining social phenomena that are complex, produced by the interaction of many factors, embedded in multiple systems, and dynamic across time' (Wasson, 2004, p. 50). Alvesson and Deetz (2000) mention that there exist different opinions about the structure of and elements included in an ethnographic study. Figure 8 portrays the three-phase design of my research, illustrating my interpretation of ethnography.

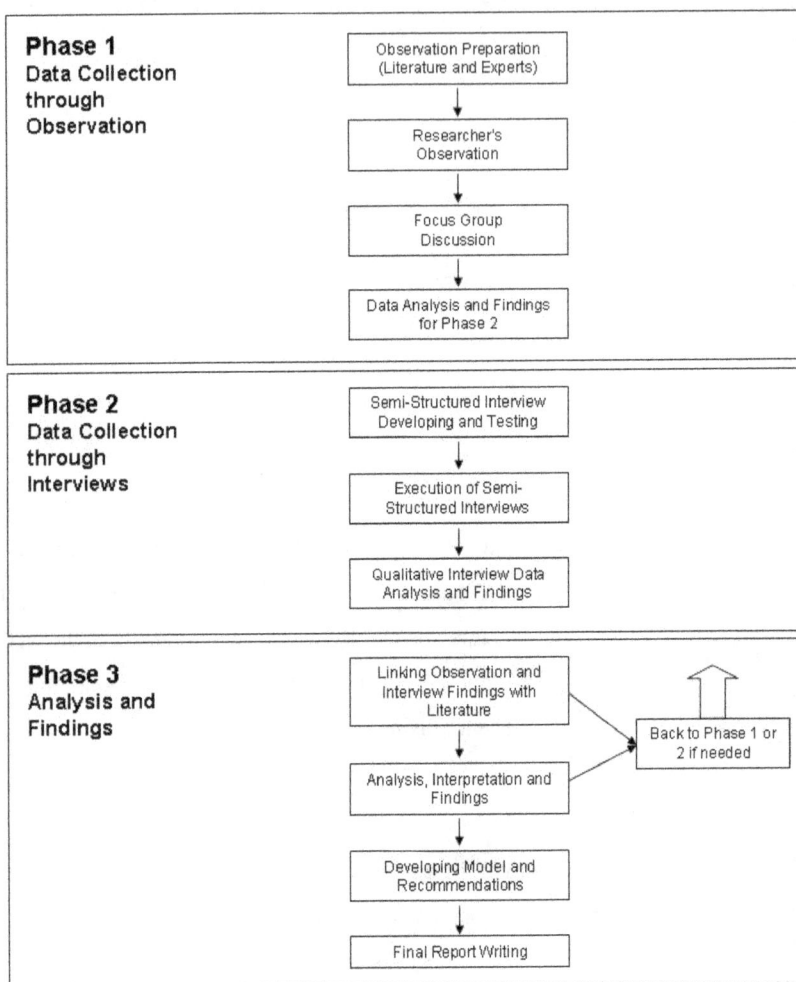

Phase 1 Data Collection through Observation	Observation Preparation (Literature and Experts)
	Researcher's Observation
	Focus Group Discussion
	Data Analysis and Findings for Phase 2

Phase 2 Data Collection through Interviews	Semi-Structured Interview Developing and Testing
	Execution of Semi-Structured Interviews
	Qualitative Interview Data Analysis and Findings

Phase 3 Analysis and Findings	Linking Observation and Interview Findings with Literature
	Analysis, Interpretation and Findings
	Developing Model and Recommendations
	Final Report Writing

Back to Phase 1 or 2 if needed

Figure 8: Three-Phase Research Design

Phase 1: Observation and Group Discussion

The first part of this dissertation explored the current situation in XYZ Europe's marketing department and revealed how the virtual marketing teams worked at that time. Phase One's objective was to understand the people and their behaviour in their particular social environment better by examining and observing their actions

46

and statements. Two methods were used: observation and group discussion (Hussey & Hussey 1997, p. 155 and 159). The purpose of the former was to unveil behavioural patters or processes the researched people themselves were not aware of since it had become routine over the years. The group discussion served as a presentation and introduction to the study and, in addition, gave information to what extent the research participants were aware of their own behaviour. Furthermore, the observations and group discussion findings were used to refine the semi-structured interview questions (Appendix B).

Phase 2: Semi-Structured Interviews

The second Phase employed semi-structured interviews (Hussey & Hussey 1997, p. 156 and 161). Thus, combined with the methods of Phase 1, this study applied a multi-method approach (observation, group discussion, and semi-structured interviews) called triangulation. Using multiple methods can increase the level of validity and reliability, one weakness of qualitative research approaches (Silverman, 2000). Hussey and Hussey (1997) consider triangulation as a possible way 'to overcome the bias and sterility of a single-method approach' (p. 74). Silverman (2000) argues that

> *by having a cumulative view of data drawn from different contexts, we may, as in trigonometry, be able to triangulate the 'true' state of affairs by examining where data intersect. In this way, some qualitative researchers believe that triangulation may improve the reliability of a single method (p. 98).*

Secondly, using different types of data collection takes the personal preferences of the team members being investigated into account: some participants may have a preference for interviews, others more for group discussions. The chosen dual-approach took the diverse preferences into account. Hence, it can be concluded that providing the participants' favourite manner of giving information can increase the quality of data collected. In addition, it allows the comparison of data on the same topic but collected in different ways. This can highlight weaknesses of one method or the other, which increases the overall quality of the research project regarding accuracy, replicability, and applicability of the findings (Hussey & Hussey, 1997; Silverman, 2000; Cavana et al., 2001).

To guide the semi-structured interviews, open-ended questions were developed in advance (Appendix B) based on information from Chapter 2 Literature Review, findings from the Research Phase 1, and finally literature about developing questionnaires and interviews (Silverman, 2000; Cavana et al., 2001; Sekaran, 2003).

Phase 3: Analysis and Findings

The last Phase analysed the findings gained from the different methods of Phase 2 and linked them to the existing theory and models. Then, the findings were transformed into practical recommendations for acting managers at XYZ (Chapter 5). After the research project, the quality and validity of the findings and recommendations can be partially measured using XYZ's internal survey. Finally, the findings were discussed separately with all the research participants via phone. Taking the objective of improving the current manner of managing virtual teams into account, I sought a consent rate (understanding the findings and agreeing with them) of at least 2/3 of the participants. A high consent rate is considered crucial for this project, since without a high acceptance of the findings and recommendations by the majority of the team members, changes leading to process and behavioural improvements could not be possible[23].

---

[23] Fifteen out of the eighteen interviewees agreed with the findings (consent rate of ~83%). Three participants did not disagree overall, but raised concerns about the generalisation of the findings.

Data Collection

Data collection including observation and interviews took place between July 2005 and December 2005. The semi-structured interviews were conducted from October 2005 until November 2005, depending on the participants' availability.

Research Participants

After written approval from XYZ Europe's marketing director, employees from XYZ Europe's marketing department (34 people in total) were approached via phone and asked for participation. Afterwards, the participant information sheets (Appendix A) were distributed via email. Prior to participating, the employees were asked to sign a consent form. It was clearly stated that participation was fully voluntary and full anonymity was guaranteed. Furthermore, no manager knows which of his or her subordinates participated in the study, preventing any negative consequences for non-participation or comments. Moreover, every XYZ employee is encouraged to freely express him or herself, as well as formulate ideas and questions without consequences (XYZ's internal code of conduct). Therefore, no team member experienced something new in being asked for his or her opinion, to question a current process, or to come up with new solutions and concepts.

Selection Criteria

The selection criteria for participants were: adult, XYZ employee, member of XYZ Europe's marketing department, only members of virtual teams, and volunteers. In addition, all of the XYZ employees interviewed were in a different team to that of the researcher. Moreover, people of the team I was leading, meaning employees reporting to me (= direct subordinates), were not interviewed in order to have a research environment free of tensions and power relationships between myself and the interviewees. Thus, voluntariness and anonymity were fully guaranteed.

Preserving Participants' Confidentiality

Since participants were assured of confidentiality, any identifying information was coded in the transcripts. Examples: The term *interviewee 1* was used instead of the real name, or *country A* or *city B* were used when participants mentioned the countries or cities where they work. Moreover, it was not possible to reveal information like differences between men/women, managers/non-managers, junior/senior, or technical/non-technical. The sample size was small and therefore this kind of information could have revealed the identity of the interviewees.

Sample Size and Sampling Method

XYZ Europe's marketing department consists of five virtual teams, 34 people in total. Eighteen interviews were conducted. Initially, it was planned to have at least 17 participants (= at least 50% of the department). All the employees of this department were invited to participate. However, since participation was fully voluntary, the research objects could not be chosen. As a result, this research had a sampling method which cannot guarantee the representativeness, and is not in any statistical sense a random sampling. Consequently, the sampling process was not influenced by any preferences of the researcher.

Data Collection Phase 1: Observation and Group Discussion

The observations were carried out taking notes in conference calls, phone calls, conversations in IM, and finally simply analysing the content of my email inbox. The ideas, patterns or processes were saved in NVivo2.0[24], a qualitative research software package. NVivo's free nodes are an ideal way to capture unstructured ideas for future use. Figure 9 shows the titles of the eleven themes gained through observation.

---

[24] NVivo homepage http://www.qsrinternational.com

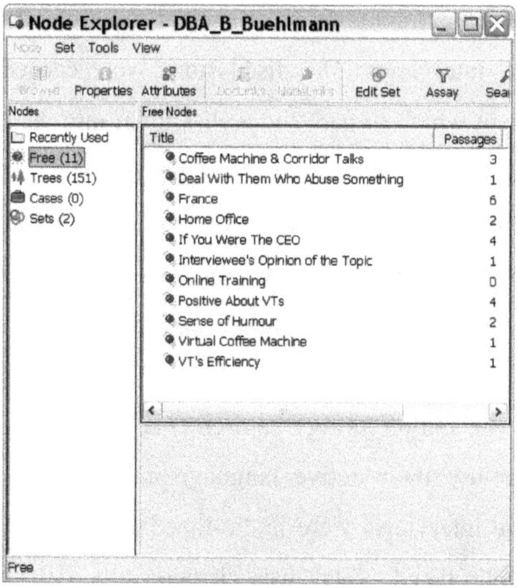

Figure 9: Observation Data in NVivo

The group discussion was held on Monday, June 13th from 14:00 until 14:20 CET[25] and was part of the regular weekly team conference call. 25 members of XYZ Europe's marketing department participated. Notes were taken and also saved in NVivo's free nodes.

Data Collection Phase 2: Semi-Structured Interviews

Prior to interviewing the actual participants, three test interviews were carried out in order to gain experience preparing and conducting semi-structured interviews. This practice assured comparable interview results with all participants from the beginning and consequently increased the quality of the data collected. For reasons of confidentiality, the test interviews were conducted with family members. Then, all the actual participants were interviewed over the phone, even those based in the same office as myself. This procedure ensured similar conditions for all people interviewed and therefore augmented the quality of data collected as well.

---

[25] CET = Central European Time = GMT + 1

51

Moreover, the philosophical assumption of critical research was taken into account when conducting the interviews. The discussions were carried out in a way that created an environment which turned 'the well-known into the exotic' (Alvesson & Deetz, 2000, p. 167). Furthermore, by applying the negation technique, participants were stimulated to think about their answers or the situation from another point of view. The interviews took between 60 and 90 minutes and were held in English, with non-native as well as native English speakers. This, however, does not represent a problem since at XYZ Europe, having a good command of the English language is one of the major hiring requirements. However, the fact that some interviewees did not use their native language is addressed in Chapter 4 Data Analysis. Finally, the interviews were audio-taped for transcription reasons. Once transcribed, the audio-taped data was irrevocably deleted for reasons of confidentiality and anonymity. Then, the transcribed text files were imported into NVivo for analysis purposes, demonstrated in Figure 9.

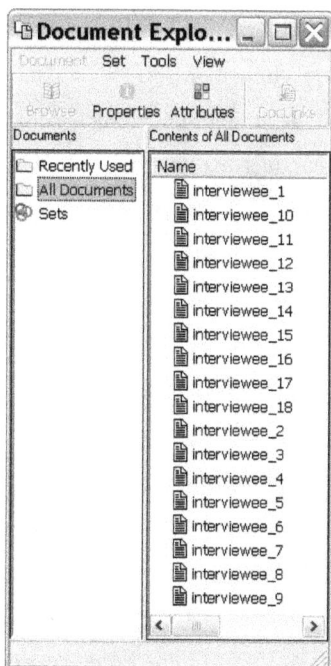

Figure 10: Transcribed Interviews in NVivo

Data Analysis

Overall, analysing qualitative data goes further than just reporting or summarising what has been said in an interview (Cavana et al., 2001). According to Robson (1993), the main challenge of qualitative data analysis is the fact that there is 'no clear and accepted set of conventions for analysis corresponding to those observed with quantitative data' (p. 370). However, the current literature provides some help based on past studies. Two concepts were considered for this research: *General Analytical Procedure* (Miles & Huberman, 1994) and *Content Analysis* (Cavana et al., 2001). The former claims methical rigour and systematic processes, due to the considerable amount of data generated in qualitative studies (Hussey & Hussey, 1997). The latter is a process of coding and categorising composed of 15 steps (Cavana et al., 2001, p. 171). In consideration of both concepts, the analysis software NVivo was chosen to conduct the data analysis. First, the way the software works (coding style, node structure, and search functions) integrates automatically the hallmarks of Miles' and Huberman's General Analytical Procedure. Second, NVivo's coding style and node structure combined with powerful search functions allows one to more easily conduct the analysis, following the 15 steps of Content Analysis. However, one needs to keep in mind that analysis software does not replace the researcher's work analysing and interpreting the data, but can only support the process itself.

Cavana et al. (2001) argue that during the analysis of qualitative data, two levels of data need to be distinguished: *manifest content* and *latent content*. According to the authors, the former is the data physically present, therefore easy to find and easy to code (e.g. words). The latter, however, underlies the physical data and consequently is more difficult to detect and code. In other words, analysing and interpreting latent content is like 'reading between the lines' (p. 175). Already in 1951 studying face-to-face groups, Bales dealt with the challenge of latent content: it is involved in *every* interpretation, by anyone, of any utterance. He concluded that it is the latent content which allows the researcher to discover the important but hidden facets of a conversation's meaning, finally permitting in-depth interpretations. Bales' findings were taken into consideration while coding and analysing the interviewees' transcripts.

Coding Process

I started the coding process making use of categories and themes developed during the literature review. However, in the course of time, new themes and patterns came to light. Hence, I conducted three rounds of coding to ensure that the new themes and patterns revealed during the coding process were included in the analysis of all transcripts. As a result, this procedure ensured a sensible level of coding quality. The final node structure can be found in Appendix C.

Validity, Reliability, and Limitations

Mehan (1979) holds that the strength of a qualitative, ethnographic field study is its ability to give a rich description of social settings. However, the author also mentions that at the same time, this strength can be considered its weakness, due to low sample sizes, anecdotal approaches, and therefore limitations regarding validity and reliability. From a positivist point of view, validity simply means truth (Silverman, 2000, p. 175). This definition is supported by Kirk and Miller (1986) as well as Hammersley (1990) who argue that validity stands for the extent to which a finding accurately represents the social phenomena studied. This is in line with the overall positivist claim that the world is adequately describable and follows universal laws, which is precisely what an interpretative understanding denies is possible. Furthermore, the same authors define reliability as the degree to which a study done by the same or different researchers yields the same results on repeated trials. Consequently, it can be argued that qualitative research is somehow limited by its very design. On the other hand, Bernstein (1983, p. 64) states that all claims to define objectivity and rationality in social science have been in vain.

I assume that for a thorough research, be it quantitative, qualitative, or a combination, concerns regarding validity and reliability need to be addressed as much as possible. Even though qualitative research acknowledges the fact that the researcher's subjectivity and bias cannot be entirely eliminated, the research design should attempt to minimise the impact on data and findings: the point is to eliminate gratuitous and unsupportable claims. Regarding my research, I recognise that only one iteration of interviews was possible within the timeframe of the DBA program. Any additional iteration might have increased the data quality and therefore the validity and reliability of the findings, either through confirming my previous findings or, in the event of contradicting outcomes, through questioning them. However, I still attempted to reach a sufficient level of validity and reliability through

- variety of methods (observation, group discussion, and semi-structured interviews)
- concepts of critical research (de-familiarisation and negation)
- three pilot interviews for testing purposes
- creating a similar environment for all interviewees (phone-based interviews only)
- three rounds of coding
- comparing findings with current literature

Therefore, I conclude that this research meets the expected academic rigour, and that its findings are a valuable contribution to the body of knowledge as well as for practitioners.

Chapter 4: Analysis and Findings

Chapter 4 provides an account of the results and key findings that principally address the preliminary question.

One point needs to be made at once concerning the interviewees' comments. All statements were exactly reproduced and accurately typed from the recording of the interview. However, the interviews were conducted in English, which is not the native language of every participant. Consequently, some citations may contain grammatical errors. In order to keep the raw data collected as precise as possible, these errors were intentionally not rectified. I argue that any alteration of the raw data could have falsified the meaning and may hence have impacted the analysis and findings.

Communication

By definition, virtual teams work across time and distance and therefore influence the way team members communicate significantly:

Our job is mainly about communication, effective communication actually.

Most comments related to communication, mainly highlighting the increased difficulty of virtual team communication:

The issue we have here at XYZ is that we spend between 90% and 95% of our time in front of the computer. We should work on the balance between working on the PC and being on the floor communicating with local people.

Communication gets more complicated, I think. Internal communication is more complex. If you build a virtual team, it means that you have people everywhere. That is much harder than if you do the same locally.

People within my own team came back saying 'we seem to be spending all your time in conference calls', which is not an effective use of anyone's time.

This resonates with the literature mentioned in Chapter 2 (Gibson & Cohen, 2003; Furst et al., 2004; Kerber & Buono, 2004; Kirkman et al., 2004; Brake, 2006). While it can be said that overall the virtual dimension adds complexity to the work environment (especially to communication), the data analysed so far does not point out *where* the difficulties lie and what are the *roots* of these complications. In regards to that matter, all interviewees agreed that a common language is an indispensable requirement for the functioning of a virtual team. However, how does a common language affect the communication in a virtual work environment? All interviewees mentioned the 'language barrier', which is, according to Soanes and Stevenson (2003), an obstacle to communication. Consequently, in this research context, a certain inhibition threshold exists when communicating in a foreign language as the following quote indicates:

The problem is sometimes that someone tries to say something in a foreign language. You know, they have the sentence in their head, translate it, and then communicate the translated sentence.

But since the team members mostly talk about familiar topics using familiar IT jargon and do not discuss complex philosophical themes, it does not seem to be of great account:

It is an issue, but it is not a big issue - as long as everybody is aware of it.

I am thinking more about what I am saying before I say it because I am aware
of the fact that there are non-native English speakers on the call. You have to
be careful using strange words or jargon.

It can therefore be concluded that the extent to which the language barrier
complicates the communication process is significantly reduced once both the
sender and the receiver of a message are aware of it. This appreciation goes along
with the recognition of the compulsory creation of a 'comfort zone' between two
communicating parties (Pauleen, 2003). According to the author, a high comfort
zone or, in other words, a strong personal relationship, is crucial for the successful
transmission of messages. His conclusion is supported by the following statement:

So it was a matter of building those relationships and establishing that
comfort factor before.

Building relationships and trust will be addressed later in this paper.

Moreover, the majority of the interviewees gave evidence that due to the overall
proficiency in English, difficulties caused by misunderstandings do not occur
because of the language barrier in the majority of cases. Such communication
problems as there are, are likely to be the ones *any* team could be confronted with,
and are therefore not specifically related to virtual teams. The following comment
illustrates this point:

Of course, the [English] language skill set is different throughout Europe. But
even in your native language, putting something down in writing is hard. I
have misunderstandings with local friends, even with my wife [participant
laughing]!

Particularly in a virtual team environment where most of the communication is electronically mediated (Gibson & Cohen, 2003), putting an idea down in writing is a frequent act of any virtual team member. Hence, it becomes an important component of virtual team communication.

Most participants raised another interesting point as to the use of a common language:

When I get one of the weird emails from France, you know regarding the translation, I just call them back and ask 'What is it what you want, because I don't understand.'

People from France usually do not like to talk on the phone, they prefer to send an email. I have heard that from other colleagues, too. They try to avoid verbal misunderstandings.

In addition, these comments are supported by the findings gained in Research Phase 1 observation (see Figure 9: Observation Data in NVivo, third node). There appears to be a strong consensus of opinion that while most participants did not associate difficulty of communication with the use of a common language in general, they clearly did so when communicating with French people (francophone). Most interviewees particularly mentioned differences in regard to sense of humour, often leading to unintentional insults and therefore unnecessary conflicts. Unfortunately, time did not allow the further investigation of this subject. Moreover, not enough French speaking participants (members of virtual teams at XYZ Europe) could be recruited. In addition, analysing all the different European cultures and their influence on communication in virtual teams is not within the scope of this research. Further research may address this. Nevertheless, it is apparently vital for virtual team members in Europe to be aware of these findings and to pay attention to the increased likelihood of communication difficulties when interacting with French colleagues.

Lastly, some interviewees indicated that native English speakers have an advantage regarding influence and power relations:

The best English speaker is often leading the discussion.

Since XYZ Europe's native English speaking employees are based in the European headquarter in UK, the issue raised is less related to the use of a common language but has more to do with power relations in connection with the place where an employee works (headquarter or branch office). Moreover, articulacy is always an advantage and a resource, or power, not merely in virtual teams. However, to pursue this issue further is beyond the scope of this paper.

Recapitulating, it can be said:

Finding 1: **In general, virtual team members at XYZ Europe do not link difficulty of communication to the use of a common language (English).**

Finding 2: **Most interviewees encountered more difficulties communicating with French colleagues.**

As a group, these practitioners believe that the increased probability of misunderstandings is the major challenge in virtual team communication:

What you write might not be what the other person will understand. If it is clear for you, it does not mean it is clear for others too. I have read [somewhere] that in a message we get, 80% is non-verbal and only 20% is verbal communication. If you only meet people virtually, you might miss 80% of the information.

This is supported by the following and very telling statement:

You know, sometimes, I piss people off, but when I go back to them and tell what I really meant, then they say 'hmm... ok, I understood it differently'.

Consequently, the virtual environment increases complexity, which causes more misunderstanding. The statements above are in line with Cramton's (2001, 2002) as well as Chawla and Krauss' (1994) findings. One way to address this challenge is to study the transmission of messages or, in other words, to investigate the 'communication channels' (Pauleen, 2003, p. 247) in virtual teams.

Communication Channels

All interviewees mentioned in one way or another the different communication channels that are available at XYZ, namely: Face-to-face (FTF), phone, phone conference, email, instant messenger, net-meeting, and video conferencing.

Most participants have a very strong preference for FTF communication:

If I can see the person in real, that is the best way.

Face-to-face is optimal. You never have enough face-to-face meetings.

As mentioned in the literature review, FTF communication transmits the most information (verbal and non-verbal) and therefore possesses the greatest level of richness and nuance of information (Gibson & Cohen, 2003), as the following comment illustrates:

If there is a problem, it is better to meet face-to-face. Even on the phone, you do not get the same attention as you have in a face-to-face meeting.

Moreover, having met FTF at least once, and if possible as early as possible, improves mutual collaboration and increases the level of commitment:

Exchanging ideas happens much more easily in a face-to-face meeting. The commitment level between people after having met is higher. Why did our team meet for the first time after 10 months? The earlier, the better.

This finding is emphasised by the very telling assertion:

We should have more FTF meetings. You are more willing to go the extra mile afterwards. You are not just an email any more. You like to open such an email much more.

The readers of emails seem to prioritise messages from people they know personally. In practice however, as the next statement reveals, the significance of FTF interactions might be underestimated or even forgotten in the beginning:

It changes completely when you see someone face-to-face - I did not expect it to be so strong. We create a virtual image of a person working with him [or her], and then, when you see the person, you might be very surprised.

Furthermore, FTF is not only perceived as fast and efficient, but may even go beyond matters directly related to the job, building relationships and trust:

Locally, you can go to the person, discuss things quickly, have a coffee, just have a chat even if you do not talk about the job – socialising.

When you meet people and then you have to call or email them later, it is always easier. The real benefit of it [the FTF meeting] is not only the meeting itself, but more the socialising part afterwards to get to know each other.

To sum up, it can be concluded that some team managers do not attach enough importance to the apparent need for FTF interactions in virtual teams. This may be due to insufficient preparation for leading a virtual team (the manager is just not aware of it), or simply because the company's organisational structure, processes, or rules (e.g. travel freeze[26] to cut costs) do not permit to foster FTF communication.

On the other hand, FTF does not seem to be the ultimate panacea for communication for companies working with virtual teams. Especially in a highly competitive environment where keeping cost as low as possible is imperative, FTF shows its limitations:

Having face-to-face meetings on a regular basis is a great option, but it is too expensive. And from personal experience, it takes time, and my time is not for free. You have to use your spare time for it.

Interviewees without family appreciated travelling to a certain extent because it allowed them to visit other cities, to make use of their foreign language skills, and to experience unknown cultures. Conversely, apart from the cost for flight, hotel, taxi, and meals, travelling is also very time-consuming (e.g. early check-in, actual travel time, delayed or cancelled flights). Particularly for employees with families, the long absence from home can be unpleasant. While most researchers primarily highlight the importance and the advantages of FTF, they often pay less attention to

---

[26] The term 'travel freeze' is often used in IT companies and signifies that during a defined period of time (like one month, or often for the rest of the current quarter), any sort of travelling is prohibited in order to reduce cost significantly. Exceptions may be granted by the president or vice-president of a region only.

its disadvantages. The cost aspect of travelling is often covered, whereas the time impact is frequently neglected. Based on interviewees' comments:

> *I had to go to Amsterdam several times already. The first time was nice, but then it became annoying, you know with x^{27} kids at home.*

and my personal experience, it seems highly doubtful that team managers always think about the implications of travelling on the private lives of their employees.

Recapitulating, it can be concluded:

Finding 3: **In a virtual team environment, FTF communication seems to be of vital importance.**

Finding 4: **However, FTF requires travel. Besides the high cost, the time impact on the employees' lives does not seem to be taken into consideration sufficiently.**

Finding 5: **A FTF meeting with all team members seems to be needed as early as possible in a work relationship, preferably at the very beginning.**

While finding 3 is not new, but confirms what the literature says (Saunders et al. (2004) for instance go so far as to call FTF the heartbeat of a virtual team), finding 4 brings another and often disregarded aspect to light with regard to travelling. Finally, finding 5 is well covered in the literature and sufficiently treated in theory (Jarvenpaa & Leidner, 1999; Kirkman et al., 2002; Gibson & Cohen, 2003; Hertel et

---

[27] The number of children could reveal the participant's identity and was therefore coded (x).

al., 2004; Beranek & Martz, 2005; Hertel et al., 2005), but apparently struggles to be implemented in practice.

The second most named communication channel is the phone. This channel is not as rich in communication as FTF (Daft & Lengel, 1984; Maruping & Agarwal, 2004):

> *On the phone, you need to understand first the social environment. It takes more time to come to the point virtually than face-to-face.*

All the same, people appreciate the ease of use (e.g. compared to the much more complicated use of video conferencing), as well as the personal touch which is often missing in electronically mediated channels:

> *I get more information faster and simpler over the phone, and it also fosters the social relationship.*

> *In a call, you have emotion involved. That is sometimes very important.*

According to the participants, emotion is often related to conflicts. Most of them consider the phone, apart from FTF, the best way to resolve a conflict:

> *That's way for important issues or disputes, I use the phone. There is no other way around. Using Outlook[28] [meaning using emails] would end in a very long email trail.*

This resonates with Gibson and Cohen's (2003) assertion that paralinguistic cues are a critical factor to reduce misunderstandings. Moreover, according to the interviewees' comments:

---

[28] Outlook is a widespread and often used email software, developed by Microsoft http://www.microsoft.com

The first couple of months [in the virtual team] were tough. I took so many things for granted and disappointed colleagues [through not meeting expectations] without knowing.

misunderstandings are the most frequent reason for conflicts. To simplify the discussion, I shall introduce the term *voice-based communication* as the umbrella term for any form of communication that includes voice, using one of the following two communication channels: FTF or phone calls. Finally, it can be argued that voice-based communication minimises the likelihood of misunderstandings and conflicts. In addition, in case of a conflict, a voice-based communication channel should be applied for a speedy resolution.

The downsides of phone calls, confirmed by the literature (Maruping & Agarwal, 2004), are the lack of a written record[29] and the fact that if one is called, one's current activity is interrupted. Interestingly, having a written record appears to be a major concern since all 18 participants came up with this as a necessity, without being prompted by a researcher's question. Finally, another weakness of phone calls is the inability to jointly look at a diagram or any other sort of graphical representation that would help understand the context faster.

Another phone-based communication channel is phone conferencing, at XYZ called 'conference call' (commonly abbreviated to 'confcall'). While a normal phone call is a 1-to-1 interaction, a conference call represents a 1-to-many conversation. At XYZ, every virtual team has at least one weekly team conference call. Some participants commented positively about conference call, highlighting its strength in sharing information, ideas, and best practices amongst team members:

---

[29] Instead of written record, some interviewees called it written proof.

Confcalls are really useful and a great tool of communication to get information.

Furthermore, a conference call is considered as a source of touch, which fosters the feeling of team togetherness (Gibson & Cohen, 2003; Filos, 2006):

It helps understand what other people do, constraints they have, you can help them and or they can help you. I feel less... [participant thinking] virtual. Strange word, isn't it? On top of that, it gives a personal touch.

On the other hand, most team members interviewed complained about the frequency as well as the length of the conference calls. Two calls or more per day of an average length of one hour are quite common. Moreover, most comments indicate that conference call participants do multitasking:

I couldn't get my work done without multitasking [talking about the frequency and durations of the calls].

or point out that not all topics covered in conference calls are of utmost importance:

Often in weekly confcalls, I don't listen to what everybody has to say, because it might not be of interest to me.

I think sometimes at XYZ we abuse that. Because it is so easy to invite eight people to the call when you actually only need three.

Such statements raise questions about the efficiency of conference calls. The participant with longest virtual team experience gave some advice:

You need to create an active call environment, trying to imitate a regular face-to-face meeting. There, you cannot hide the multitasking. At the end of the day, we are adults. We try to stick to the rules we agreed, but you know... Like project management, in the beginning, you define a set of rules.

Moreover, most interviewees felt that participating in a conference call is sometimes an unofficial 'must' for political reasons, indirectly imposed by team managers:

To be honest, I think it is sometimes more a political thing to be on a confcall.

In summary, conference calls are overall seen as a very useful and helpful tool. However, the way they are currently applied in practice is seen as having too many drawbacks and as having a negative influence on the virtual team collaboration. Besides, behavioural rules seem to be missing. The implications of multitasking are discussed later in the paper.

Prior to introducing the next findings, I refine my definition of voice-based communication, adding phone conference (changes to the first definition are highlighted in bold type):

Voice-based communication is the umbrella term for any form of communication that includes voice, using one of the subsequent **three** communication channels: FTF, phone calls, or **conference call**.

Finding 6:   Voice-based communication lacks a written record.

Finding 7:   Virtual team members seem to appreciate a written record after communicative interactions.

69

Finding 8: Voice-based communication seems to reduce the likelihood of misunderstandings significantly.

Finding 9: Voice-based communication should be applied to resolve conflicts quickly.

Maruping and Agarwal (2004) hold that 'The technology-mediated nature of communication increases the likelihood of ... misunderstandings' (p. 971). However, the authors' statement does not disprove finding 8 as might appear at first sight, even though voice-based communications also falls into the category of technology mediated communication. In cases where FTF is not an option for any reason, voice-based communication seems to be the most appropriate choice by virtue of its ease of use and its ability to transmit the significant paralinguistic cues:

I get more information faster and simpler over the phone, and it also fosters the social relationship.

The subsequent four communication channels analysed fall into the category of electronically mediated communication (abbreviated EMC), as they are all based on specific applications (software) and rely on the company's network.

Netmeeting (a web-based presentation software developed by Microsoft) combines the conference call with a slide presentation, and eliminates the previously discussed disadvantage of phone-based communication: the inability to jointly look at a diagram or any other sort of graphical representation. Netmeeting is widespread at XYZ, most of the weekly team meetings make use of this software. No relevant negative characteristics of this application were raised in the interview. However, some interviewees mentioned that it is simpler to send the presentation slides in an email to the netmeeting participants than to upload the presentation slides onto the netmeeting server, especially in case of spontaneous and unplanned meetings.

By far the most used communication channel is email. It undoubtedly possesses valuable features like easy transmission of files as attachments or having a written record:

The best about email is that you always have something written, you know the send date, who sent it, and who received it.

but most comments clearly had a negative touch. Among the various answers, three major concerns were identified. First[30], the volume of emails:

More and more, I get frustrated because on some days I get over a hundred emails a day. I was out of the office for a week. I came back and had seven hundred unread emails.

If people write an email, they think if they add as many people as possible, it will resolve the problem faster, but that is not the case. I mean it is a behavioural problem.

While just a few team members make use of email rules[31], the majority of them do not work, or no longer work, with rules by virtue of the constantly changing nature of XYZ's organisational structure. Both local and virtual teams are partially or fully reorganised once or sometimes even twice a year. As a result, most interviewees claimed that to keep pace with these changes would require them to change the rules on a regular basis. This procedure is felt to be too complicated and time-consuming.

Applying the philosophical assumptions of critical research, I asked the following question trying to incorporate elements of Alvesson and Deetz's (2000) concept of

---

[30] The sequence of the concerns presented does not indicate the order of importance.
[31] Email rules permit automatically forwarding messages and/or storing them in subfolders.

de-familiarisation: 'What about the idea of limiting the number of emails per week per person?' While at first most participants perceived it as a great idea (probably because it would directly reduce the number of emails received), they suddenly realised that it would limit the amount of emails they send, and were therefore no longer in favour of this approach. The subsequent question was intended to make the participants aware of circumstances and facts they were not conscious of: When asked to open the sent-folder[32] in Outlook, the majority of interviewees were very surprised with the number of emails they had sent, between 40 and 70 emails per day.

Finding 10: **Most virtual team members experience difficulties dealing with the considerable volume of emails.**

Finding 11: **Most virtual team members were not aware of the number of emails they send on a daily basis.**

While finding 10 is widely accepted in the literature (Gibson & Cohen, 2003; Pauleen, 2003; Hertel et al., 2005; Filos, 2006), finding 11 could not be identified in the literature reviewed to date. However, its significance is that it may be used to show employees that, by sending numerous emails per day, they are also part of the problem of the inundation of emails.

The second concern refers to email privacy and future readers of a message, as two statements illustrate:

I make an example: It is really bad if there is a communication between two people and suddenly the other guy puts other people on copy or forwards the email to someone else. You know, it may be a manager... [participant

---

[32] The sent-folder in Outlook contains all the emails sent unless the employee intentionally deletes them.

thinking]. You see the issue? Then suddenly a third party can read your communication which you first thought is purely a 1-to-1 communication.

There is a danger in forwarding or copying people... It is similar to talking behind someone's back. So it was not agreed in the beginning to send this email chain to another person. It has happened to me several times.

The latter exemplifies the anxiety in a figurative manner. Talking behind someone's back is obviously undesirable and uncomfortable. Moreover, it has a political dimension since an email may be used against you. In summary, the sender of an email loses control over the message sent, and can in no way influence the future utilisation. After some reflection, it became clear that one of email's strengths, having a written proof, may also be its major drawback.

Finding 12: **The sender of an email loses control over the message and its future utilisation.**

Even though this finding is not particularly related to virtual teams, since it may occur in local teams working with email too, team members should be made aware of this circumstance and its possible consequences in order to minimise misunderstanding and conflict risks to themselves and others. In virtual teams, however, this phenomenon becomes even more important as email is the most used communication channel.

Finally, the third drawbacks springs from questions of responsibility and ownership of the tasks mentioned in the email. In the current email setting at XYZ, it is not possible to refuse an email; it just shows up in the inbox. Whether the receiver can be held responsible for the content and its tasks received, however, is an unanswered question as it is nowhere defined:

If you send an email, you need to clarify the responsibilities, and write something like 'please confirm'. It is like a deal or a contract; it is only valid if the other person agrees.

People just cascade and forward emails and actions required.

As a result, employees can become overwhelmed with tasks, requests, and responsibilities. Some interviewees mentioned symptoms of stress as a direct consequence, in conjunction with difficulties of prioritisation:

People do not prioritise what they send and to whom, and they don't include deadlines like "until the end of the day or week."

Emails, I get about 100 a day - plus IM, it is sometimes too much. I feel lost, don't know where to start.

While XYZ provides an intensive two-week induction training for every new employee, dealing with the above-mentioned challenges is not covered in XYZ's preparatory course.

Finding 13:   Emails may cause a conflict of responsibility.

Finding 14:   Most virtual team members struggle with prioritisation in regard to the amount of emails.

While articles in the literature in most instances investigate the causes, the implications for practitioners are often omitted. Stimulated by the critical research environment applying Alvesson & Deetz's (2000) concept of negation, one interviewee came up with a helpful suggestion:

In general, I think people should use the rule "if you send an email, you will probably not get an email back right away". So if you really need an answer back or for important things, you need to call... [participant thinking] or IM[33] him.

This comment contributes to the body of knowledge in two ways. First, it seems that Alvesson & Deetz's (2000) concepts intended to create a critical research environment were successful and yield new insights (finding 11 and 15). Second, even though the rule stated in the previous comment might appear rather simple at first sight, it may be of paramount importance for practitioners as it signifies at least a first attempt to solve a daily and major practical concern. Further research in a real-world environment is needed in order to test and further develop this insight.

Finding 15: **Alvesson & Deetz's concepts intended to create a critical research environment could be applied and appear to be functional.**

Instant Messenger (IM) is a rather new, emerging communication channel. At XYZ, IM has been in use for approximately two years. IM's initial purpose was to offer a synchronous communication, similar to the phone, but with writing instead of speaking. This research, though, revealed that applied in a real-world business environment, IM serves primarily another major purpose:

I use instant messenger the most to see whether this person is online or not. Then I know that I can call or email him.

---

[33] Over the last years, the abbreviation of Instant Messenger IM became a verb within XYZ's virtual teams. E.g. He tried to IM his boss.

Interestingly, interviewees unanimously agreed that the feature to see who is online is of the utmost importance. Moreover, IM is highly appreciated by most participants on account of its ability to quickly share short messages:

We use messenger which is really, really good because you don't have to read a lot. You can ask short questions really quickly.

Instant messenger is great if you just need a yes or no.

Further, for reasons of ease and pace, the majority of the virtual team members preferred IM to phone for short messages. Instead of searching and dialling a phone number, IM permits to quickly connect to someone via a simple double-click. Moreover, some interviewees pointed out additional advantages like lower cost (no phone charge), or its ability to quickly send a link to a file stored on XYZ's intranet.

Finding 16: **In a virtual business environment, the cardinal feature of IM is its ability to indicate which team members are online and therefore reachable.**

Finding 17: **Most virtual team members exchange rather brief messages via IM.**

Finding 18: **IM permits contacting team members more quickly and at lower cost compared to the phone.**

On the other hand, IM also lacks the written proof that most virtual team members consider necessary:

You discuss something in instant messenger, then, they often say "send me an email". They want to have the written track to be covered.

In addition, IM may cause conflicts in regard to response time:

And sometimes, IM is misused in a way that people expect an immediate response.

The cause of this phenomenon could be rapidly identified. While XYZ lays down an explicit code of conduct for emails, which requires that employees respond to an email within 24 hours, no distinct rule exists in regard to IM. Moreover, Finding 18 is a positive characteristic of IM, but it may, at the same time, become a disadvantage. By virtue of pressure of time, IM's ease of use may tempt some people to contact multiple team members simultaneously to get a rapid answer or clarification, without having to think about it themselves. As a result, some participants felt that they are subjected to a great deal of work and disturbance by team members abusing IM. Nobody mentioned concerns regarding privacy or perceived level of control. Consequently, and in summary, it can be argued that it is not only IM that should have set rules to ensure proper and efficient communication, but every communication channel.

Finding 19: To improve virtual team interactions, an official code of conduct for each communication channel should be applied.

The last communication channel, video conferencing, is by far the most infrequently used option:

I don't know whether we have one here, to be honest.

Almost nobody uses it. It is first complicated to book it, and then not easy to use it.

From a theoretical point of view, one could argue that video conferencing should be one of the preferred communication channels as it transmits visual and paralinguistic cues. The interviewees' comments, however, contradict this theoretical assumption, naming complexity of use as a reason. Future research might clarify this point.

According to Pauleen (Pauleen, 2003), the selection and use of communication channels is crucial to a virtual team's success. These findings are in accordance with the media-richness theory (Daft & Lengel, 1984), which investigates the information richness of each communication channel and graphically compares each channel's assets and drawbacks (Maruping & Agarwal, 2004, p. 978). While there are numerous articles dealing with the various communication channels (Daft et al., 1987; Daft & Lengel, 1988; Maruping & Agarwal, 2004), I have not found the phenomenon of using more than one communication channel when interacting with team members to accomplish a task in the literature reviewed to date. This study, however, indicates that all participants often combined communication channels:

I use instant messenger the most to see whether this person is online or not. Then I know that I can call or email him.

I do not have the luxury to ask the same question twice. For instance, I send an email and then I pick up the phone and call. For me, that is the most efficient way.

Two frequent and typical patterns of combining communication channels could be identified: email-phone and email-IM. I assume that virtual team members combine channels in order to compensate for the disadvantages of a particular channel, e.g. written proof. Further, I think that the interviewees are either consciously or subconsciously aware of each channel's shortcomings. I interpret *consciously aware* if a person knows a channels' features (e.g. from school) and chooses them accordingly, whereas *unconsciously aware* if a person acts unknowingly based on prior experiences, in other words based on tacit knowledge (Williamson, 1985). My interpretation is based on the fact that none of the participants were told to combine communication channels; the phenomenon just occurred naturally over the years.

Finding 20: Virtual team members often combine communication channels. The most frequent combinations of communication channels are email-phone and email-IM.

When writing finding 20, the word triangulation immediately crossed my mind. I see an analogy between finding 20 and triangulation discussed in Chapter 3, as both cases act on the same maxim: applying multiple methods may increase the quality of the outcome. Consequently, suitable for this and maybe future research contexts, the term *triangulation of communication channels* seems apt: triangulation of communication channels occurs when more than one communication channel is utilised in order to more successfully accomplish a communicative interaction.

Finally, an interesting causal relationship relevant to practice was unveiled analysing the transcripts. Table 8, drawn from the interviewees' comments, compares the order of preference of communication channels versus the order of frequency of use.

Table 8: Comparison of Preference versus Frequency of Use of Communication Channels

Order of Preference	Order of Frequency of Use
1. FTF 2. Phone Call 3. Netmeting, Conference Call, IM 4. Email 5. Video Conferencing	1. Email 2. Conference Call 3. Netmeeting, IM 4. Phone Call 5. FTF 6. Video Conferencing

Interpreting Table 8 revealed a surprising connection: there seems to be a mainly inversely proportional relationship between the team members' preference of a communication channel, and the frequency a channel is used. Excluding video conferencing, since it is virtually never used at XYZ, the two most preferred channels FTF and phone call are the least frequently used ones, while the least preferred channel email is the most common.

> **Finding 21:** **Overall, there seems to be a mainly inversely proportional relationship between the team members' preference of a communication channel and the frequency a channel is used.**

Although the literature addresses preferences of communication channels (Pauleen, 2003; Maruping & Agarwal, 2004; Hertel et al., 2005), the topics (preference and frequency of use of a communication channel) are treated separately. Comparing them side-by-side and highlighting the inversely proportional relationship between preference and frequency of use, however, has not been found in the literature reviewed to date. Finding 21 describes the current situation, that the richest and most preferred channels are the least frequently used, but does not offer an immediate solution (how the richest and most preferred channels could be utilised more often). Nevertheless, it seems to be a valuable insight for theory and practice as it may serve as a starting point for future improvement processes or further research.

Trust

Most interviewees raised trust-related topics without being prompted. This indicates that, at least to a certain degree, they were conscious of trust related concerns in one way or another, or that they had done an MBA[34] or read literature on the topic of trust and virtual teams:

Trust is an important thing; it has something to do with moral, too.

If there is no trust, you cannot work with this guy.

If there is a low level of trust, you might not share your pains and issues which is needed to fix them.

While most of the interviewees had not previously come across the distinction of trust into initial trust and building trust, the majority of them accepted the existence of initial trust after a short explanation and even found it a surprising insight:

Hmmm... [participant thinking] I think the initial trust thing is very true. You do it right away when you see or just even hear a person.

Finding 22:   **Most virtual team members were not aware of the existence of initial trust, but eventually quickly came to acknowledge that is was something important and valuable.**

Moreover, in accordance with conclusions of McKnight et al. (1998), most participants believed that the initial trust level largely depends on prior experiences and the cultural setting. The discussion of initial trust automatically prompted some virtual team members to raise the question of how to build trust:

---

[34] However, only one participant holds a degree in Business Administration (MBA). Further, the participants stated that they had not read literature about virtual teams prior to the interviews.

Locally, I would first have a coffee - a real one, of course [participant laughing] - and chat a little. After a face-to-face introduction, trust is growing quite fast.

This resonates with finding 5 and corresponds well with Kirkman's et al. (2002) assertion that an early FTF interaction correlates positively with team productivity as well as team members' satisfaction, and finally may have a positive influence on the level of trust. Furthermore, their view is widely supported in the literature (Jarvenpaa & Leidner, 1999; Zheng et al., 2002; Hertel et al., 2004). Moreover, a few comments supported Hertel's et al. (2005) assumption that non-job-related communication facilitates the trust building process further.

Finding 23: **Early FTF interactions, even if not job-related, may facilitate the virtual team members' trust building process.**

All statements analysed revealed that FTF communication seems to be a very effective way of building trust, but is not indispensable:

If the execution you agreed on is good, I guess you can build trust the same way as you can in a local team. But it takes longer.

If you stick to your promises, like a fair giving-and-taking, it builds trust, however more slowly.

You need proofs of trust, and this comes with the work experience.

All three statements may directly or indirectly indicate a tendency towards the existence task-based trust (Mayer et al., 1995; Kirkman et al., 2002) and lead to the next finding.

Finding 24: **In virtual teams, living up to agreed expectations may facilitate the trust building process even without FTF interaction.**

Finding 24 was further supported by the participant with the most virtual team experience, who emphasised the significance of a fast response, even if it is not the final answer:

> *The first thing you need to do is being responsive in a timely manner. Responding fast is crucial. I always respond to all my emails the same day, even though I might not be able to give the final answer, just to let him know that I am on it.*

So far, this paragraph has discussed how the level of trust can be increased in virtual teams, according to the participants and the literature reviewed. From a practical point of view however, the fast-paced work environment calls for building trust rapidly. The literature revealed, confirmed by my own findings, that FTF communication seems to establish trust the fastest:

> *To get it effective, you almost have to start with a face-to-face meeting to build it [trust] up fast.*

One statement indicated not only that FTF interactions foster trust, but also discussed the practical advantage of building trust as early as possible in a virtual team's life cycle:

> *[In FTF team meetings] we work but we also chat, spend a nice evening out, and socialise. That is building the foundation and trust. Back home, we can use this trust and <u>focus on the work instead of trust building.</u>*

The last part of the citation '... and focus on work instead of trust building' is interesting, as it points out that initial FTF interactions may free up time afterwards, possibly leaving virtual team members more time to execute their daily tasks.

From an interpretivist point of view, one may question whether trust can truly be built by mechanical methods as the largely positivist literature believes. I would argue that to augment the level of trust, person A rather has to 'earn' person B's trust. I think that building trust can probably not be imposed by a person and therefore does not seem to be a unidirectional process, but appears rather to require a mutual acceptance and might therefore be more likely a bidirectional process. Before person B 'accepts' person A's trust-building efforts, the level of trust might not increase significantly or not at all. This correlates to a certain extent with finding 7 which states that most interviewees usually demand a written record of agreements. Why is this? Do they not trust the other team members? Did the trust-building efforts not work as well as hoped? Although dealing with the question whether trust can be built or needs to be earned is beyond the scope of the present study, I suggest that people executing trust-building measures should at least take this question into account.

Finding 25: **People executing trust-building measures should think about whether trust can be built by mechanical methods or whether trust needs to be earned by the other person. If trust needs to be earned, trust-building measures might need to be adapted.**

As this dissertation is also meant to focus on practice and to come up with recommendations or guidelines for acting managers (therefore coloured by positivism), I have tried to visualise the advantage of early FTF interactions in regard to trust. An easily understandable graphical representation illustrating the benefit of early FTF interactions may prove to be useful in practice because it allows virtual team managers to justify the high travel and accommodation cost of FTF meetings. Figure 11 compares how the level of trust may rise over time in virtual teams with an early FTF interaction versus without. The left graph portrays the significant increase of trust owing to early FTF interactions. On the other hand, the right one presents the lower levels of trust in virtual teams without FTF interaction. However, it nevertheless indicates that even without FTF meetings, the level of trust may increase in the course of time, even if more slowly than with FTF. Related to the literature reviewed, the left graph represents interpersonal trust whereas the left one symbolises task-based trust (Mayer et al., 1995; Kirkman et al., 2002).

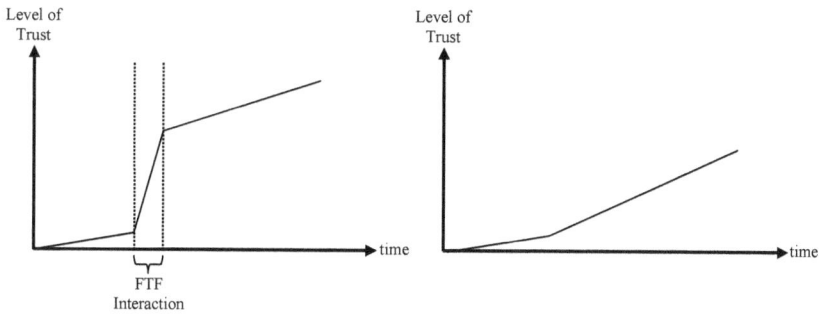

Figure 11: Comparing Trust Building With and Without FTF Interaction

The aim of this comparison is to offer the reader a simple visualisation of the advantage of early FTF interactions in regard to trust. Therefore, the graphs do not contain any measures. Moreover, neither the gradient angle nor the length of the lines intend to indicate any information based on mathematical calculations and are thus not discussed further.

A note concerning the right graph: The little elbow was incorporated intentionally as I suppose that task-based trust may not increase linearly, but may ascend at a different rate after a while. This assumption is based on some participants' experience that without initial FTF interactions, the team-building progress and the outcomes were rather moderate in the early stage of the team's life cycle. After a while, though, they felt that the team progressed much faster. This phenomenon resonates well with Tuckman's (1965) Four-Stage Model. The left part of the right graph's curve represents the less effective stages 1 and 2 (Forming and Storming), whereas the continuation after the elbow portrays the more productive Stages 3 and 4 (Norming and Performing). Consequently, it can be said that Tuckman's simple stage model was confirmed in this research.

Combining both curves, Figure 12 finally attempts to visualise the trust level benefit of early FTF meetings. The resulting grey area may serve, to a certain degree, as a measure of trust gained.

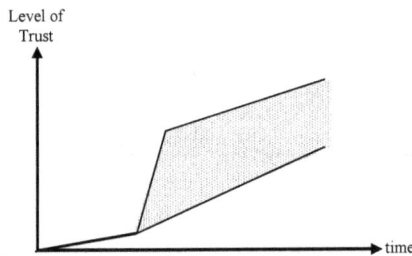

Figure 12: Attempt to Visualise FTF's Advantage in Building Trust

Even though the advantage could not be quantified monetarily, Figure 12 may nevertheless convince companies to invest in early FTF meetings. Financially speaking, the grey area indicates the return on investment of early FTF meetings relating to the level of trust in virtual teams.

If FTF interaction is not possible in the beginning, Pauleen (2003) argues that the phone is the second most rapid manner to build trust because it allows team members to '… pick up paralinguistic clues, such as tensions or uncertainty…' (p. 247). By virtue of these clues, the author claims that the phone is rich enough to get to know people. Thus, the use of phone builds trust. Consequently, since trust building is particularly crucial in the beginning of a virtual team's life, it can be concluded that:

Finding 26: **In early stages of a virtual team's life, FTF or phone-based communication seems to be preferable to EMC.**

Finding 26 then may lead to a further conclusion: in a later stage of a virtual team's life, when a higher level of trust has been established, EMC may be sufficient to communicate successfully:

Once you know the other guy more, you can interpret even short messages in emails or IM better. I have kind of a picture of this person in mind when reading his email. That helps.

It seems that when communicating electronically (via email or IM), having a picture of the team-mate in mind, in conjunction with positive previous work experiences, may help interpret written messages better. As a result, fewer misunderstandings might occur.

Finally, the mention of pictures leads to the last topic discussed in this paragraph: the use of emoticons (examples of frequently used emoticons are a smiling face ☺ or an unhappy face ☹). Most interviewees frequently use emoticons in their written communications:

I use them [emoticons]. They allow me to stress the meaning of my message.

In other words, emoticons may partially compensate for the lack of verbal and non-verbal cues in emails and IM conversations. Further research may examine to what degree emoticons can improve the written communication.

Virtual Team Skills

Beside the already discussed difficulties of communication in virtual teams, the majority of the interviewees took up a largely positive stance on working in a virtual team. Their statements revealed advantages like more freedom and independence:

You can work from home.

I work more independently now, and when it suits me. You know, I have family.

Moreover, skills crucial to virtual team environments were identified, such as a higher degree of maturity,

[Virtual team members] They must be more mature and on top can build teams much faster. Overall, [the virtual team] it is something positive.

better organised,

You have to manage things yourself. You plan and organise more. This makes you stronger.

and more structured:

You become more structured. Example: You have regular weekly meetings you need to prepare for. You have to know where you need to be and what you need to do.

In summary, it seems that a successful virtual team requires team members with a specific skill set. Even though a high level of maturity or good organisational skills are also beneficial to local teams, they seem to be of particular importance in a virtual team environment. Kirkman et al. (2002) emphasise the 'good balance of technical and interpersonal skills' (p. 74) and suggest that companies should adapt their recruiting process accordingly. Moreover, in order to assess the applicant's phone-based communication skills, the authors believe that at least one job interview should be conducted on the phone. Finally, all participants collectively agreed on the importance of a well-balanced skill set for virtual teams. After being asked whether the virtual team skill set was specifically mentioned in their C.V., most answered similarly to the following statement:

> *Never thought about adding it to the C.V., but I think we should do it. I will update my C.V. [Participant thinking] You know what? Man! They even asked me for this stuff in the XYZ interview!*

This citation indicates that not all virtual team members are aware of the need for a specific skill set in virtual team environments.

Finding 27: **The virtual team environment seems to require team members with a specific virtual team skill set (more mature, better organised, better structured, and independent working style).**

Finding 28: **Companies might think about adapting their recruiting process when hiring new virtual team members.**

Multitasking

A further distinctive attribute of virtual teams is their tendency to 'multitasking'. All interviewees reported on their experiences related to it. Overall, multitasking appears to be perceived negatively in this study due to: reasons of respect,

I think it [multitasking] is rude. You don't respect the other guy on the confcall. It goes back to the level of a person.

reasons of inefficiency in phone-based communication,

I think it is probably the worst thing we do. You often have to repeat stuff because people say "Sorry, what was the question?"

owing to fatigue,

I stopped multitasking in confcalls. It was too tiring. Mentally tiring I mean. I got headaches.

or because of general concerns of the quality of the outcomes:

We should not do it [multitasking]. I get interrupted all the time. You do everything but nothing right.

To sum up, it can be said that the research revealed mainly negative aspects of multitasking.

Finding 29:   Overall, most interviewees disrelished multitasking.

Finding 29 confirms and contradicts the literature at the same time. While in line with Gibson and Cohen's (2003) assertion, it partially disagrees with Wasson's (2004) conclusions. She holds that 'multitasking can enhance employee productivity when properly managed' (p. 47). Consequently, further research is required to understand how multitasking at XYZ Europe could be beneficial to the business.

Models

Models are clearly coloured by positivism, as they try to generalise and represent universal laws and connections. In this research context, models are utilised to bridge theory and practice, that is, to help practitioners understand a socially complex real-world environment better, knowing that models can never entirely and correctly represent reality.

Tuckman's (1965) Stage Model already demonstrated its usefulness in the paragraph on Trust, assisting in understanding Figure 11. Furthermore, a connection could be made between the level of trust and the stage number. While Stages 1 and 2 (Forming and Storming) possess a lower level of trust as well as a lower growth rate of trust, Stages 3 and 4 (Norming and Performing) posses a higher level of trust and trust may grow faster (see Figure 11). Due to task-based trust, this connection seems also to be true in the event a virtual team cannot meet FTF in the beginning.

Finding 30: **Tuckman's stage model has proved itself and could be connected to the existence of task-based trust.**

Based on finding 24 and now also finding 30, this research indicates for a second time a tendency towards the existence of task-based trust, which seems to be a relevant element of virtual team management to be taken into account in theory and practice.

With regard to the Virtual Team Dynamics model introduced by Kerber and Buono (2004), I suggest three alterations based on findings of this research. First, the authors consider lavish information flow as a centripetal force bridging the team together. I disagree, and argue that, supported by finding 11 as well as the literature (Gibson & Cohen, 2003; Pauleen, 2003; Hertel et al., 2005; Filos, 2006), the arrow should be inverted (see circle number 1 in Figure 13). Virtual team members face a great deal of difficulties coping with overabundant information, especially with email.

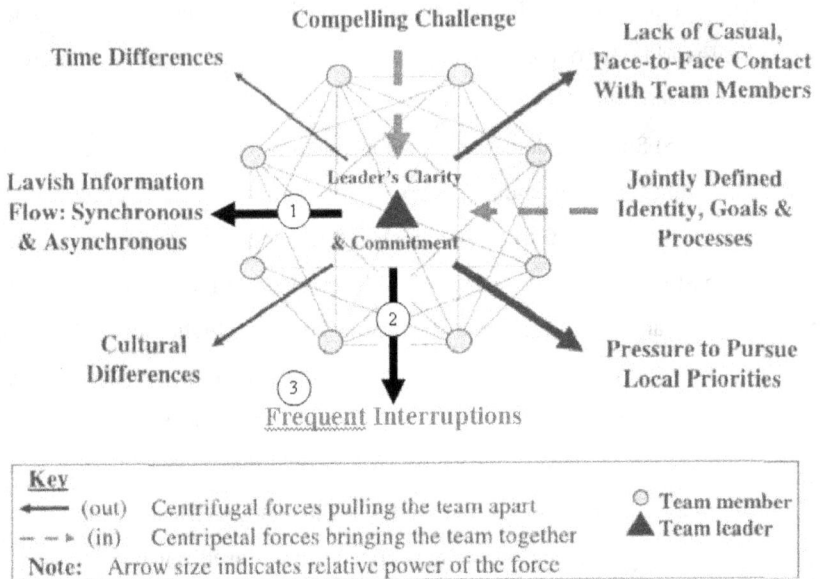

Time Differences

Compelling Challenge

Lack of Casual,
Face-to-Face Contact
With Team Members

Lavish Information
Flow: Synchronous
& Asynchronous

Leader's Clarity
& Commitment

Jointly Defined
Identity, Goals &
Processes

Cultural
Differences

Pressure to Pursue
Local Priorities

Frequent Interruptions

Key
◄─── (out) Centrifugal forces pulling the team apart   ○ Team member
─ ─ ► (in)   Centripetal forces bringing the team together   ▲ Team leader
Note: Arrow size indicates relative power of the force

Figure 13: Altered Model of Virtual Team Dynamics

Second, I removed the label 'Performance Management' and its corresponding arrow. Albeit performance management in virtual teams is certainly more difficult because of the geographical dispersion and the increased complexity, nevertheless, I believe that this handicap may be, at least partially, compensated by findings 27 and 28. Moreover, especially in an environment like XYZ, where all teams (virtual or collocated) are led applying the "Management by Objective" approach, performance management becomes less exigent as weekly reports automatically indicate where a team or an individual employee stands compared to the objectives. Even though performance management is certainly a valid element of virtual team management, I replace it with "Frequent Interruptions" and add a centrifugal arrow (see circle 2 and 3) as I believe that it is more relevant to a virtual team environment. Consistent with finding 29, I argue that being frequently interrupted correlates negatively with the virtual team's outcomes. In accordance with the majority of the interviewees, multitasking is often the root cause of interruptions, indicated in the very telling statement below:

Sometimes, it gets just crazy. You are in a confcall, keep getting emails, someone calls you on the other line and then, another employee contacts you via IM. [Participant breathing deeply] That's too much, really.

Hence, these interruptions may represent a centripetal force, tending to pull the team apart. Appendix D contains the original, as well as the altered model, on one page and therefore allows easy comparison. As regards the thickness of the altered arrows: while Kerber and Buono (2004) utilise the arrows' thickness as an indicator of the strength of each phenomenon, it was beyond the scope of this study to formulate valid information about the phenomena's effect in comparison to other phenomena. As a result, both the thickness and the length of the two arrows altered do not represent any information. Future research is required to provide meaningful results in this regard.

Finding 31: **In most instances, the Virtual Team Dynamics model could be confirmed by the findings of this study. However, three alterations were made in order to reflect and incorporate findings 11, 27, 28, and 29.**

This chapter revealed 31 findings considered as relevant to practice. The findings were discussed and compared with the literature. The next and final chapter is intended to transform these findings into major conclusions and applicable recommendations for practitioners concerned with virtual team management.

Chapter 5: Conclusions and Recommendations

Answering the central research question, the fifth and last chapter takes the findings from Chapter 4 and attempts to transform them into applicable recommendations for practice in the light of XYZ Europe (or closely similar organisation). The following recommendations do not claim to be universally applicable, or to be entirely true for any virtual team at XYZ Europe. These suggestions are not meant to undermine advantages of virtual teams, such as few regulations and unbureaucratic working methods, freeing the potential and creativity of team members; they are intended to serve as a starting point for reflection for acting managers of virtual teams at XYZ Europe, and possibly elsewhere. Moreover, Chapter 5 highlights this study's contribution to the body of knowledge, addresses further its limitations, and finally offers suggestions for future research.

Implications for Practice

The following recommendations are based on interviewees' suggestions, proposals found in the literature, and findings of Chapter 4. Considering the scarce time of people working in fast-paced real-world environments, I framed the key recommendations in order to allow practitioners to access the key information directly and quickly.

Recruiting Virtual Team Members

After the phases of job analysis and job design to have a clear understanding of the positions to be filled, building a virtual team usually starts with the hiring process (Goodbody, 2005). In the case where a team leader takes over an existing team, hiring becomes relevant as soon as the first team members leave and need to be replaced. It is crucial for the success of a virtual team to have team members that are able to cope with the increased complexity and the communication challenges. Therefore, based on finding 27 and 28, I suggest:

> **Managerial recommendations**
> - The recruiting process should be adapted when hiring virtual team members considering the specific virtual team skill set.
> - A portion of the job interview should be held over the phone to test the applicant's capabilities in phone-based conversations.
> - A portion of the job interview, even if only for a few minutes, should be based on email communication to test the applicant's capabilities in clear and intelligible writing.

Once the virtual team *members* are identified and available, the *team* itself needs to be created.

Establishing a Team Idendity

Applying Tuckman's (1965) model, the 'Forming' stage should serve to establish a 'shared team identity' (Furst et al., 2004, p. 15). In order to foster the team's cohesion and to create a feeling of togetherness, the authors suggest a team-specific logo. Interestingly, this idea has arisen from the interviews as well. The creation of the team logo itself could be the first joint team task. Like passports indicating the nationality of a person, the team logo may serve as a sort of identification of team membership of employees.

> **Managerial recommendations**
> - A team-specific logo may support the feeling of togetherness.
> - The creation of the team logo could be part of the first team meeting.

In addition, the 'Norming' stage is supposed to make team members aware of each other's competencies, and should moreover result in a clear and mutually agreed team mission. However, this may prove to be difficult as it is in a virtual team's nature to have rare face-to-face interactions. Pauleen (2003) asserts that the selection and use of the various communication channels are crucial for the successful relationship building process of a virtual team.

Selection of Communication Channels

The advantages and disadvantages of the communication channels available in most virtual teams have been thoroughly discussed in previous chapters. To achieve the objectives of the 'Norming' stage named above, face-to-face interactions seem to be indispensable. Therefore, based on findings 3 and 5, I suggest:

> **Managerial recommendation**
> - A face-to-face meeting with all team members should take place as early as possible of a work relationship, preferably in the very beginning.

Face-to-face communication is the richest of all communication channels and should hence be employed on a regular basis. However, drawbacks like high costs (for the company) and time spent (for the employee) should be considered; especially the latter, as it is often overlooked. Consequently, on the basis of finding 4, I suggest:

> **Managerial recommendation**
> - Virtual team managers should consider the time impact of business trips on employees' private life, especially if they have family.

Thanks to its ability to transmit paralinguistic cues, voice-based communication is the second richest communication channel[35]. It significantly reduces the likelihood of misunderstandings compared to electronically mediated communication, and should therefore be utilised as often as possible. However, the lack of a 'paper trail' is its considerable disadvantage. For archiving reasons, email is perfectly suited to compensate for this weakness. Example: After a phone call or a conference call, one person may write a summary email and send it to all participants. Consequently, and based on findings 6, 7, 20, and 21, I suggest:

Managerial recommendations

- Communication channels should be combined to compensate for each channels' weaknesses.
- Useful combinations are email-phone and email-IM to address the missing written proof in phone-based or IM communication.

While email's strengths, like the possibility of attaching files or archiving, are highly appreciated by practitioners, it contains a well hidden danger that numerous users are not conscious of. No email sender can in any way influence the future utilisation of the message. Example: a team member writes an email with a delicate content, perhaps a comment about the team manager, to another team member. The receiver could easily forward this message to the team manager, without letting the sender know. Moreover, the content of an email may even be altered before forwarding to a third person. As a result, the final receiver of the email trail may read a modified message of the initial sender. Hence, based on finding 12, I suggest:

---

[35] Taking into account that video conferencing would be even richer, but is virtually never used by virtue of its complicated handling.

> **Managerial recommendation**
> - While writing an email, virtual team members should keep in mind that the sender completely loses control over the message and its future utilisation.

Furthermore, emails may cause conflicts of responsibility amongst team members as orders, tasks, or instructions can easily be sent to another person. This issue deserves particularly high attention as email seems to be the most used communication channel in most virtual team environments. Moreover, dealing with prioritisation and archiving the overabundant emails presents an additional problem to team members. In conclusion, based on findings 13 and 14, I suggest:

> **Managerial recommendation**
> - As emails may cause conflicts of responsibility as well as present a problem in regards to prioritisation and archiving, directions for use should be established.

The geographical dispersion is one of the key characteristics of virtual teams. As a result, team members cannot see whether another team member is already in the office and working on his or her desk. IM offers an easy and affordable solution to this problem. In one glace, it can be determined who is already online and working at their desk. Therefore, it may be concluded that IM augments the productivity of a virtual team, as it prevents team members from calling and recalling other team members in vain. In summary, based on findings 16 and 18, I suggest:

> **Managerial recommendations**
> - IM provides the possibility of seeing which team members are attainable, and should therefore be installed on all personal computers of virtual team members.
> - IM permits contacting team members more quickly, without having to dial a long international phone number, and at lower cost as compared to the phone.

Recapitulating, it can be said that while every communication channel has its justification in a certain situation, face-to-face communication is needed as early as possible in a virtual team's life. In reality however, virtual team managers often have difficulties getting approvals for face-to-face meetings due to the high cost of travelling. The next paragraph is intended to provide some help in this subject.

Justifying Face-to-Face Meetings to Senior Management

Most of today's senior managers gained their management experience in non-virtual team environments. However, many of them now find themselves in a virtual team situation without having a theoretical background through studies. As a result, the senior management may not always be aware of the importance of initial face-to-face interactions in virtual teams. This may be one of the reasons why virtual team managers often struggle with obtaining flight and travel approvals. In such situations, the graphs in Figure 12 and Figure 13 may prove to be rather useful in explaining why early face-to-face meetings are crucial to a virtual team's success, and justifying the high costs associated with them. Moreover, convincing arguments like "… a well functioning team will have a positive impact on the customer and employee satisfaction" may augment the chance of obtaining the approvals. In case a financial manager needs to be convinced, the same graphs may also serve as justification in conjunction with a more financially speaking approach like "The grey area indicates the return on investment of early face-to-face meetings relating to our overall success and the customer satisfaction. We do not want to disappoint Wall Street's analysts[36]." Consquently, based on findings 3, 5, 23, and 26, I suggest:

Managerial recommendations

- The graphs provided in this paper may serve to justify the high cost of early face-to-face meetings to senior management.
- In case a finance manager needs to be convinced for approvals, a more financial approach and vocabulary should be chosen.

Addressing the Dual-Membership

In the majority of cases, virtual team members are also embedded in the local structure and are therefore members of local, non-virtual team as well. As discussed in Chapter 2, the dual-membership results in a more complex work environment (Hertel et al., 2005), since virtual team members are also supposed to meet local expectations. Thus, both the virtual and the local team manager need to agree on the employees' objectives and priorities in order to prevent stressed and overloaded virtual team members. A company may simplify and support this by establishing firm-wide norms on how responsibilities should be distributed between local and virtual teams in general. Therefore, I suggest:

Managerial recommendations

- Both virtual and local team managers need to agree on each virtual team member's objectives and priorities.
- A company-wide solution is preferable.

---

[36] XYZ Inc. is listed at the New York Stock Exchange (NYSE) and has to report on a quarterly basis. Not to disappoint Wall Street's analysts relates to XYZ's stock price.

Addressing Multitasking

Multitasking seems to be a major concern of virtual team members. It can be perceived as rude, and therefore as displaying a lack of mutual respect, and causes frequent interruptions, or even leads to stress and headaches, to mention just a few of the drawbacks mentioned by the interviewees. Even though the literature claims that multitasking may increase the productivity of a team 'when properly managed' (Wasson, 2004, p. 47), the potential negative consequences should be taken into account and addressed. One interviewee came up with a reasonable idea: a virtual team manager should establish an environment in which 'saying no' is allowed to prevent multitasking. More precisely, refusing to pick up the phone or to start a conversation in IM due to a currently ongoing task should not result in negative consequences of any kind for the team member. Consequently, based on finding 29, I suggest:

> **Managerial recommendation**
> - To prevent the potential negative consequences of multitasking, a work environment should be established in which 'saying no' is allowed.

As already stated in previous paragraphs, the complexity of virtual teams calls for norms or rules in order to facilitate a smoother and more successful collaboration.

Establishing Rules and a Code of Conduct

The need for rules in virtual teams is also supported in the literature. Furst et al. (2004) emphasise that establishing rules should take place as early as possible to prevent unnecessary conflicts in the initial team building process. Therefore, a code of conduct regarding the selection of communication channels, aspects of multitasking, the dual-membership, and perhaps other elements depending on the company, should be introduced in the very beginning. The act of creating the code of conduct itself could be part of the team building activities, be it face-to-face or in a conference call. Every team member should be encouraged to participate, as it may foster the team cohesion and create a feeling of togetherness. Moreover, this procedure may increase the future acceptance of the agreed upon team rules. For reasons of simplicity however, a company-wide solution is preferable. Once the set of rules is established, it should be continuously developed, taking future cognition and learning into account. Finally, it is the team managers' decision what is included in the code of conduct. Without claiming to be complete, the following list may serve as a starting point.

- How communication channels should be applied and combined.
- A list of abbreviations or terms (jargon) that should be used.
- File templates, e.g. for reports or agendas for team meetings.
- Whether multitasking is accepted or not. If yes, what are the limitations?
- How and when feedback should be given.
- Escalation steps in case of conflicts
- 'Laptop down'[37] rule for phone calls and phone conferences

Consequently, based on findings 10, 11, 17, and 19, I suggest:

Managerial recommendations
- A code of conduct should be established as early as possible to simplify the team's future collaboration, and to minimise the likelihood of conflicts between team members.
- Ideally, all team members should participate in creating the set of rules to increase its future acceptance.

---

[37] 'Laptop down' is an expression often used in the IT field and means that the laptop should be closed during the conversation to prevent the interlocutors from being distracted.

Building Trust

Establishing trust as early as possible in the development of a virtual team seems to be critical to the functioning of the group (Kirkman et al., 2002; Maruping & Agarwal, 2004; Goodbody, 2005) and facilitates the handling of conflicts that cannot be entirely prevented when people work together. As discussed in Chapter 4, trust can be divided into interpersonal trust and task-based trust. While the former should mainly be built during the initial team building activities, the latter is supposed to emerge over time if team members live up to the mutual expectations. In order to live up to expectations and to prevent conflicts, the code of conduct named above can come into play again. Therefore, it can be concluded that a causal relationship exists between the existence of the code of conduct and building task-based trust. Team managers may utilise Figure 12 and Figure 13 to make employees aware of the fact that trust can be built remotely and without regular face-to-face interactions. Furthermore, companies may think about including trust related topics in their induction programs for new employees.

In conclusion, based on findings 22, 23, and 25, I suggest:

Managerial recommendations

- To start with a high level of (interpersonal) trust, virtual teams should have substantial face-to-face interactions during the initial team building activities.

- Virtual team managers should demonstrate to their team members how a strict observance of the mutually agreed upon code of conduct correlates well with building (task-based) trust.

- Companies should include topics relating to building trust in virtual teams in their induction trainings for new employees.

Addressing the Language Barrier

In light of virtual teams' nature, team members are geographically dispersed and do thus not always have the same native language. As a result, virtual teams need a common team language. Nowadays, English is predominant in the IT industry. Team members not communicating in their mother tongue may or may not present a communicative problem, depending on each team member's command of the common language. This research revealed that at XYZ, the use of English does not present a serious difficulty overall. However, communicating with French colleagues seems to be trickier. Even though it was beyond the scope of this paper to investigate why the majority of the interviewees felt this to be the case, it is nevertheless an indication that team managers should pay attention to this possible source of misunderstandings and conflicts.

In regard to native English speakers, they may still possess a certain linguistic power advantage over the non-English speaking team members if difficult vocabulary is applied. Therefore, it may be wise to discuss this potential cause of conflict in 1-to-1 sessions with native English speakers. In addition, the possibly unintentional abuse of native English speakers' linguistic power may also be a useful topic for induction trainings. Consequently, based on finding 1 and 2, I suggest:

Managerial recommendations

- At XYZ Europe, virtual team managers should in particular pay attention to team members in France. The likelihood of misunderstandings and conflicts when communicating appears to be higher than with team members from other European countries.

- Native English speakers should be made aware of their linguistic advantage and pay attention to their vocabulary when communicating with non-native English speaking team members.

Addressing Cultural Differences

Working in a multi-national virtual team means dealing with people that may have diverse cultural backgrounds. As discussed in Chapter 2, culture can be seen as a shared understanding and sense making, unofficial rules, general behaviours, and non-stated beliefs of a cultural entity (Schein, 1993). Applied to practice, unequal non-stated beliefs and rules may result in unforeseen misunderstandings and conflicts. Thus, the cultural variety might negatively impact communication amongst virtual team members. Gibson and Cohen (2003) suggest that team members should 'discuss cultural differences and similarities openly' (p. 418). In regard to XYZ Europe, most interviewees mentioned jokes as a frequent example of causes of conflict and emphasised the importance of knowing the other team member's cultural settings. Nowadays, paperbacks about cultural dissimilarities are available and give the reader a short introduction to most cultures' dos and don'ts. Moreover, some research participants proposed posting so-called 'cultural one-pagers' on the XYZ intranet, accessible to every employee. Finally, cultural differences could also be covered in a company's induction training or during team building events.

> **Managerial recommendations**
> - Cultural differences present a source of conflict and need therefore to be addressed as early as possible.
> - The topic may be covered in induction training and team buildings events.

Managing Conflicts

The paragraphs and recommendations previously mentioned in this chapter are all intended to prevent misunderstanding and conflict in virtual teams. However, in a fast-paced and multi-cultural work environment, disagreement, quarrels, and arguments may occur nevertheless. In practice, employees far too often try to resolve problems via email, a communication channel lacking the crucial paralinguistic cues. As a result, employees complain about extensive email trails and a long resolution time, especially if emotions are involved. In such situations, richer communication channels like face-to-face or voice-based communication should be utilised. Companies might even think about measuring the use of phone and email to oversee progress. Therefore, on the basis of findings 8 and 9, I suggest:

> **Managerial recommendations**
> - Face-to-face or voice-based communication should be utilised to settle conflicts.
> - Virtual team managers should encourage team members to use the phone as often as possible.
> - Because of its lack of paralinguistic cues, email should not be used to resolve disagreements.

Early Trainings

The participants' statements revealed that most of them were not aware of the full complexity of virtual teams. At the end of each interview, the participants were asked whether, and to what degree, the interview would influence their future work:

I will think more before I do something. And I will use the phone more often for sure.

Consequently, it can be concluded that simply discussing the topic made the participants think about the virtual team environment in general, allowed insight into and appreciation of certain problems related to this emerging work environment, and even generated ideas how to tackle them. To benefit from this company-wide, as already mentioned in previous paragraphs, virtual team training should take place as early as possible. The findings of Chapter 4, as well as the recommendations in this chapter, may serve as base to structure such training for all virtual team members. Depending on a company's structure, the virtual team training may be part of the regular induction session, or be set up separately.

> **Managerial recommendation**
> - As not all virtual team members might be aware of the peculiarity of a virtual team environment, specific training for virtual team members is required as early as possible.

Furthermore, as finding 27 indicates, working in a virtual job environment calls for a specific skill set. Thus, the role of a virtual team manager also entails a different skill set compared with collocated team managers. Consequently, training tailored to virtual team managers' needs is desirable. The content may build upon the above-named course for virtual team members, but may also include and discuss underlying connections and relationships. The two models discussed and examined in this paper (Tuckman, 1965; Kerber & Buono, 2004) may be incorporated in the training as they illustrate the life cycle, as well as the relationships, in virtual teams.

Taking all of the above into account, it can be concluded that training seems to be crucial. It makes sense to prepare all stakeholders of virtual teams for the virtual team environment. Thus, based on findings 30 and 31, I suggest:

> **Managerial recommendations**
> - By virtue of the dissimilar work conditions in virtual teams, specific training for virtual team managers is required.
> - The two models discussed in this paper may serve as a basis for the virtual team manager training.

Contribution to the Body of Knowledge

In summary, this work contributes to the body of knowledge in eight ways. First, I extended prior work on virtual teams by testing current models in a real-world environment. Based on the research findings, the Virtual Team Dynamics Model (Kerber & Buono, 2004), for instance, was modified, while Tuckman's (1965) Stage Model has confirmed itself without major alterations. Second, Alvesson and Deetz's (2000) suggestions for critical management research were applied in a real-world environment and seem to be functional. Third, task-based trust could be identified in this study, and may therefore confirm the existing literature. Fourth, the already familiar concept 'degree of virtualness' (Gibson & Cohen, 2003) was further developed by visualising the dual-membership of virtual team members. Fifth, this study revealed the mainly inversely proportional relationship between the team members' preference of a communication channel, and the frequency a channel is used. While previous research has discussed the richness of, and team members' preferences among, communication channels, a comparison with the frequency of use of the communication channels has not been found in the literature reviewed. Sixth, the gap in the literature, the need for testing the theoretical assumptions gained from experimental settings under real-life conditions (Hertel et al., 2005), could be addressed. Seventh, this study questions whether trust can be truly built (as believed by the largely positivist literature about virtual teams), or whether it needs to be earned. Finally, this applied research project yields down-to-earth suggestions for practitioners in virtual team environments.

Limitations and Suggestions for Further Research

Overall, due to limitations of program length and word count, not all of the relevant topics could be dealt with thoroughly. Throughout the paper, where appropriate, I pointed out when a topic was beyond the scope of this research. In addition, this paragraph names further limitations and suggestions for future research.

Cultural and Industry Dimension

First, the cultural dimension of virtual team is a relevant theme on which to elaborate. Especially in a European context with dozens of cultures and languages, the cultural dimension becomes more important compared to a virtual team in the United States of America, for instance. Second, further research might attempt either to extend the number of research firms within the same industry sector, or to seek a basis for broader cross industry conclusions.

Total Cost of Communication Channels

Third, the total costs caused by the use of communication channels were neglected. However, by virtue of the steadily increasing price pressure in the IT industry, the cost advantage of certain communication channels may become relevant quite soon. While some participants stated that email, for instance, is free, it is obvious that this communication channel is clearly not without cost, as all electronically mediated communication channels are linked to expenditures of infrastructure and maintenance.

Virtual Team Leadership

Fourth, the importance of virtual team leadership became apparent during the research. Virtual team managers face a more complex job environment than managers of collocated teams. Future research may focus on the virtual team manager as a major unit of analysis and continue Pauleen's (2003) work. In this connection, Filos (2006) argues that job rotation, in other words every team member taking on the manager role for a definite period of time, correlates positively with virtual teams' performance, as well as with the overall job satisfaction. The concept of job rotation in virtual teams is currently not utilised at XYZ Europe, but might be a fruitful extension to this study.

Employment in Low-Wage Countries

Fifth, globalisation and virtual teams eventually lead to more employment in low-wage countries. As a result, some employees receive a significantly lower salary for the same job performance. Neither the literature reviewed, nor the interviewees, even though some of them work in low-wage countries, touched this delicate topic. While prices for local products are doubtless lower in emerging countries, prices for proprietary articles, cars, or international flights, for example, are the same as in Western countries. Consequently, some employees have a lower buying power for the same job performance. Therefore, jealousy and resentment to a certain degree are inevitable. Further research might take this element into consideration.

Virtual Team Model

Sixth, the Virtual Team Dynamics Model (Kerber & Buono, 2004), altered in Chapter 4, offers opportunities for further research. As mentioned, the thickness of the arrows (indicating the strength of a phenomenon) could not be determined during this project. In addition, the model altered would benefit from more empirical testing to confirm, or refute, the modifications proposed.

Research Participants and Trust Building

Seventh, I am aware of the possibility that the responses I received from the interviewees may not be based on pure experience, but may be coloured by orthodoxies of various kinds. Finally, the question whether trust can be built through specific and tailored measures, or if trust needs to be earned, may be part of future research.

Overall Conclusions and Contributions

I hope to have achieved the initially stated aim to improve the understanding of both the nature of virtual teams in general (theory), and of the challenge of managing virtual teams in European IT companies (practice). It proved possible either to confirm or question existing theoretical knowledge. As to the practical implications of the research, acting virtual team managers can easily access the specifically highlighted managerial recommendations (which are clearly identified) without being required to do extensive reading, a relevant consideration in a fast-paced industry. For those who are interested in better understanding the rationale behind the suggestions, Chapter 4 provides an account of the results and key findings of the research itself.

References

Alderfer, C. 1977, 'Group and intergroup relations' in *Improving the quality of work life*, (Eds: J.R., H. & Suttle, J. L.), Pacific Palisades, Goodyear, CA, pp. 227-296.

Alge, B. J., Ballinger, G. A. & Green, S. G. 2004, 'Remote control', *Personnel Psychology*, vol. 57, no. 2, pp. 377-411.

Alvesson, M. & Deetz, S. 2000, *Doing critical management research*, SAGE Publications, London.

Andres, H. P. 2006, 'The impact of communication medium on virtual team group process', *Information Resources Management Journal*, vol. 19, no. 2, pp. 1-17.

Atkinson, P. & Hammersley, M. 1994, 'Ethnography and participant observation' in *Handbook of Qualitative Research*, (Eds: Denzin, N. & Lincoln, Y.), Sage, Thousand Oaks, CA, pp.

Baker, G. 2002, 'The effects of synchronous collaborative technologies on decision making: a study of virtual teams', *Information Resources Management Journal*, vol. 15, no. 4, pp. 79-94.

Becker, M. C. 2001, 'Managing dispersed knowledge: organizational problems, managerial strategies, and their effectiveness', *Journal of Management Studies*, vol. 38, no. 7, pp. 1037-1051.

Bell, B. S. & Kozlowski, S. W. 2002, 'A typology of virtual teams: implications for effective leadership', *Group & Organization Management*, vol. 27, no. 1, pp. 14-49.

Beranek, P. M. & Martz, B. 2005, 'Making virtual teams more effective: improving relational links', *Team Performance Management*, vol. 11, no. 5, pp. 200-213.

Bernstein, R. J. 1983, *Beyond objectivism and relativism*, University of Pennsylvania Press, Pennsylvania.

Brake, T. 2006, 'Leading global virtual teams', *Industrial & Commercial Training*, vol. 38, no. 2/3, pp. 116-121.

Brown, H. G., Scott-Poole, M. & Rodgers, T. L. 2004, 'Interpersonal traits, complementarity, and trust in virtual collaboration', *Journal of Management Information Systems,* vol. 20, no. 4, pp. 115-137.

Burtha, M. & Connaughton, S. L. 2004, 'Learning the secrets of long-distance leadership', *KM Review,* vol. 7, no. 1, pp. 24-27.

Cackowski, D. 2000, 'Object analysis in organizational design: a solution for matrix organizations', *Project Management Journal,* vol. 31, no. 3, pp. 44-51.

Cascio, W. F. 2000, 'Managing a virtual workplace', *Academy of Management Executive,* vol. 14, no. 3, pp. 81-90.

Cavana, R. Y., Delahaye, B. L. & Sekaran, U. 2001, *Applied business research: qualitative and quantitative methods,* John Wiley & Sons, Milton, Australia.

Chawla, P. & Krauss, R. M. 1994, 'Gesture and speech in spontaneous and rehearsed narratives', *Journal of Experimental Social Psychology,* vol. 30, no. 6, pp. 580-601.

Collis, J. & Hussey, R. 2003, *Business research. a practical guide for undergraduate and postgraduate students,* Palgrave Macmillan, London.

Cramton, C. D. 2001, 'The mutual knowledge problem and its consequences for dispersed collaboration', *Organizational Science,* vol. 12, no. 3, pp. 346-371.

Cramton, C. D. 2002, 'Finding common ground in dispersed collaboration', *Organizational Dynamics,* vol. 30, no. 4, pp. 356-367.

Cummings, L. L. & Bromiley, P. 1996, 'The organizational trust inventory OTI' in *Trust in Organizations: Frontiers of Theory and Research,* (Eds: Kramer, R. M. & Tyler, T. R.), Sage, Thousand Oaks, CA, pp.

Daft, R. L. & Lengel, R. H. 1984, 'Organizational information requirements, media richness and structural design', *Management Science,* vol. 32, no. 5, pp. 554-571.

Daft, R. L. & Lengel, R. H. 1988, 'The selection of communication media as an executive skill', *Academy of Management Executive,* vol. 2, no. 3, pp. 225-232.

Daft, R. L., Lengel, R. H. & Trevino, L. 1987, 'Media symbolism, media richness, and media choice in organizations', *Communication Research,* vol. 19, no. 1, pp. 52-90.

Dani, S. S., Burns, N. D., Backhaus, C. J. & Kochhar, A. K. 2006, 'The implications of organizational culture and trust in the working of virtual teams', *Engineering Manufacture,* vol. 220, no. 6, pp. 951-960.

Davidow, W. H. & Malone, M. S. 1993, *The virtual corporation: structuring and revitalizing the corporation for the 21st century,* Harper Business, New York.

DeSanctis, G. & Jackson, B. M. 1994, 'Coordination of information technology management: team-based structures and computer-based communication systems', *Journal of Management Information Systems,* vol. 10, no. 4, pp. 85-110.

Drucker, P. F. 1988, 'The coming of the new organization', *Harvard Business Review,* vol. 66, no. 1, pp. 45-53.

Duarte, D. L. & Snyder, N. T. 2001, *Mastering virtual teams strategies, tools, and techniques that succeed,* Jossey-Bass, San Francisco, California.

Filos, E. 2006, 'Smart organizations in the digital age' in *Integration of Information and Communication Technologies in Smart Organizations,* (Eds: Mezgár, I.), Idea Group, Inc., Hershey, PA, USA, pp. 1-37.

Finholt, T. A. 2002, 'Collaboratories', *Annual Review of Information Science and Technology,* vol. 36, no. 1, pp. 73-107.

Furst, S. A., Reeves, M., Rosen, B. & Blackburn, R. S. 2004, 'Managing the life cycle of virtual teams', *Academy of Management Executive,* vol. 18, no. 2, pp. 6-22.

Gable, G. 1994, 'Integrating case study and survey research methods: an example in information systems', *European Journal of Information Systems,* vol. 3, no. 3, pp. 112-126.

Gibson, C. B. & Cohen, S. G. 2003, *Virtual teams that work: creating conditions for virtual team effectiveness,* Jossey-Bass, San Francisco, CA.

Goodbody, J. 2005, 'Critical success factors for global virtual teams', *Strategic Communication Management,* vol. 9, no. 2, pp. 18-21.

Gould, D. 2002, *'Virtual organization',* Electronic Source, last viewed March 15th, 2006 http://www.seanet.com/~daveg/vrteams.htm

Grenier, R. & Metes, G. 1995, *Going Virtual: moving your organization into the 21st century,* Prentice Hall, Upper Saddle River, NJ.

Grosse, C. U. 2002, 'Managing communication within virtual intercultural teams', *Business Communication Quarterly,* vol. 65, no. 4, pp. 22-38.

Hackman, J. R. 1987, *The design of work teams,* Prentice Hall, Upper Saddle River, NJ.

Hale, R. & Whitlaw, P. 1997, *Towards the virtual organization,* McGraw-Hill, London.

Hammersley, M. 1990, *Reading ethnographic research: a critical guide,* Longmans, London.

Handy, C. 1995, 'Trust and the virtual organization', *Harvard Business Review,* vol. 73, no. 3, pp. 40-50.

Hertel, G., Geister, S. & Konradt, U. 2005, 'Managing virtual teams: a review of current empirical research', *Human Resource Management Review,* vol. 15, no. 1, pp. 69-95.

Hertel, G., Konradt, U. & Orlikowski, B. 2004, 'Managing distance by interdependence: goal setting, task interdependence, and team-based rewards in virtual teams', *European Journal of Work & Organizational Psychology,* vol. 13, no. 1, pp. 1-28.

Hosmer, L. T. 1995, 'Trust: the connecting link between organization theory and philosophical ethics', *Academy of Management Review,* vol. 20, no. 2, pp. 379-403.

Hussey, J. & Hussey, R. 1997, *Business research: a practical guide for undergraduate and postgraduate students,* Palgrave Macmillan, New York.

Jarvenpaa, S. L. & Ives, B. 1994, 'The global network organization of the future: Information management opportunities and challenges', *Journal of Management Information Systems,* vol. 10, no. 4, pp. 25-57.

Jarvenpaa, S. L., Knoll, K. & Leidner, D. E. 1998, 'Is anybody out there? Antecedents of trust in global virtual teams', *Journal of Management Information Systems,* vol. 14, no. 4, pp. 29-64.

Jarvenpaa, S. L. & Leidner, D. E. 1999, 'Communication and trust in global virtual teams', *Organization Science,* vol. 10, no. 6, pp. 791-816.

Joy-Matthews, J. & Gladstone, B. 2000, 'Extending the group: a strategy for virtual team formation', *Industrial and Commercial Training,* vol. 32, no. 1, pp. 24-29.

Katzenbach, J. R. & Smith, D. K. 1993, *The wisdom of teams: creating the high-performance organization,* Harper Business, New York.

Katzy, B. R. 1998, 'The virtual enterprise' in *Handbook of life cycle engineering: concepts, models and tools,* (Eds: Gutiérrez, A. M.; Sánchez, J. M.; Kusiak, A. & Molina, A.), Kluwer Academic Publishers, Dordrecht, The Netherlands, pp.

Kerber, K. W. & Buono, A. F. 2004, 'Leadership challenges in global virtual teams: lessons from the field', *SAM Advanced Management Journal,* vol. 69, no. 4, pp. 4-10.

Kirk, J. & Miller, M. L. 1986, *Reliability and validity in qualitative research,* Sage Publications, London.

Kirkman, B. L., Rosen, B., Tesluk, P. E. & Gibson, C. B. 2004, 'The impact of team empowerment on virtual team performance: the moderating role of face-to-face interaction', *Academy of Management Journal,* vol. 47, no. 2, pp. 175-193.

Kirkman, B. L., Rosen, B., Tesluk, P. E., Gibson, C. B. & McPherson, S. O. 2002, 'Five challenges to virtual team success: lessons from Sabre, Inc', *Academy of Management Executive,* vol. 16, no. 3, pp. 67-79.

Knoll, K. & Jarvenpaa, S. L. 1995, 'Learning virtual team collaboration', *Hawaii International Conference on System Sciences,* Hawaii.

Kuprenas, J. A. 2003, 'Implementation and performance of a matrix organization structure', *International Journal of Project Management,* vol. 21, no. 1, pp. 51-62.

Lipnack, J. & Stamps, J. 1997, *Virtual teams: reaching across space, time, and organizations with technology,* John Wiley & Sons, London.

Maruping, L. M. & Agarwal, R. 2004, 'Managing team interpersonal processes through Technology: a task-technology fit perspective', *Journal of Applied Psychology,* vol. 89, no. 6, pp. 975-990.

Mayer, R. C., Davis, J. H. & Schoorman, F. D. 1995, 'An integrative model of organizational trust', *Academy of Management Review,* vol. 20, no. 3, pp. 709-734.

McKnight, D. H., Cummings, L. L. & Chervany, N. L. 1998, ' Initial trust formation in new organizational relationships', *Academy of Management Review,* vol. 23, no. 3, pp. 473-490.

Mehan, H. 1979, *Learning lessons: social organization in the classroom,* Harvard University Press, Cambridge, MA.

Miles, M. B. & Huberman, A. M. 1994, *Qualitative data analysis,* Sage, Thousand Oaks.

Mowshowitz, A. 1997, 'The switching principle in virtual organizations', *EJOV Electronic Journal of Organizational Virtualness,* vol. 1, no. 1, pp. 6-18.

Mowshowitz, A. 1999, 'Virtual organizations', *Communication of the ACM,* vol. 40, no. 9, pp. 30-37.

O'Hara-Devereaux, M. & Johansen, R. 1994, *Globalwork,* Jossey-Bass, San Francisco, CA.

Palmer, J. & Speier, C. 1997, 'A typology of virtual organizations: an empirical study', *Association for Information Science,* Indianapolis.

Pauleen, D. J. 2003, 'An inductively derived model of leader-initiated relationship building with virtual team members', *Journal of Management Information Systems,* vol. 20, no. 3, pp. 227-256.

Prasad, P. 1997, 'Systems of meaning: ethnography as a methodology for the study of information technologies' in *Information Systems and Qualitative Research*, (Eds: Lee, A. S.; Liebenau, J. & DeGross, J. I.), Chapman and Hall, London, pp. 101-118.

Punch, K. F. 2000, *Developing effective research proposals,* Sage Publications, London.

Ragin, C. C. & Becker, H. S. 1992, *What is the case? Exploring the foundations of social inquiry,* Cambridge University Press, Cambridge.

Robson, C. 1993, *Real world research,* Blackwell, Oxford.

Roebuck, D. B., Brock, S. J. & Moodie, D. R. 2004, 'Using a simulation to explore the challenges of communication in a virtual team', *Business Communication Quarterly,* vol. 67, no. 3, pp. 359-367.

Saunders, C., Van Slyke, C. & Vogel, D. R. 2004, 'My time or yours? Managing time visions in global virtual teams', *Academy of Management Executive,* vol. 18, no. 1, pp. 19-31.

Schein, E. H. 1993, *Organizational culture and leadership,* Jossey-Bass, San Francisco, CA.

Schermerhorn, J. R., Hunt, J. G. & Osborn, R. N. 2000, *Organizational behavior,* John Wiley & Sons, New York.

Scott, S. G. & Einstein, W. O. 2001, 'Strategic performance appraisal in team-based organizations: one size does not fit all', *Academy of Management Executive,* vol. 15, no. 2, pp. 107-116.

Sekaran, U. 2003, *Research methods for business: a skill building approach,* John Wiley & Sons, USA.

Shapiro, C. & Varian, H. R. 1999, *Information rules: a strategic guide to the network economy,* Harvard Business School Press, Boston, MA.

Silverman, D. 2000, *Doing qualitative research: a practical handbook,* SAGE Publicatons, London.

Soanes, C. & Stevenson, A. 2003, *Oxford Dictionary of English,* Oxford University Press, Oxford.

Strader, T. J., Lin, F. R. & Shaw, M. J. 1998, 'Information infrastructure for electronic virtual organization management', *Decision Support Systems,* vol. 23, no. 1, pp. 75-94.

Sy, T. & Côté, S. 2004, 'Emotional intelligence: a key ability to succeed in the matrix organization', *Journal of Management Development,* vol. 23, no. 5, pp. 437-455.

Sy, T. & D'Annunzio, L. S. 2005, 'Challenges and strategies of matrix organizations: top-level and mid-level managers' perspectives', *Human Resource Planning,* vol. 28, no. 1, pp. 39-48.

Townsend, A. M. & DeMarie, S. M. 1998, 'Virtual teams: technology and the workplace of the future', *Academy of Management Executive,* vol. 12, no. 3, pp. 7-29.

Tuckman, B. W. 1965, 'Development sequence in small groups', *Psychological Bulletin,* vol. 63, no. 1, pp. 384-399.

Venkatraman, N. & Henderson, J. C. 1998, *Sloan Management Review,* vol. 40, no. 1, pp. 33-49.

Wasson, C. 2004, 'Multitasking during virtual meetings', *Human Resource Planning,* vol. 27, no. 4, pp. 47-60.

Williamson, O. E. 1985, *The economic institutions of capitalism: firms, markets, relational,* Collier Macmillan, London.

Wilson, S. 2003, 'Forming virtual teams', *Quality Progress,* vol. 36, no. 6, pp. 36-41.

Zheng, J., Veinott, E. S., Bos, N., Olson, J. S. & Olson, G. M. 2002, 'Trust without touch: jumpstarting long-distance trust with initial social activities', *CHI Letters,* vol. 4, no. 1, pp. 141-146.

Appendix A: Participant Information Sheet

University of South Australia

International Graduate School of Business

Participant Information Sheet

Study Title	Study Conducted by
Managing Virtual Teams: A Case Study at XYZ Europe	Beat A. Buhlmann

Invitation to Participation

All members of XYZ Europe's marketing team are kindly invited to participate in this internal study regarding virtual team management.

Purpose of the Study

The overall aim of this applied research is to improve the virtual team management at XYZ Europe. This research project is composed of two parts. The first objective is to analyze the current manner of virtual team management at XYZ Europe in order to better understand key elements and current processes. The second objective is then to improve the way virtual teams are managed at XYZ. Finally, XYZ managers should get a simple model or recommendations helping to more efficiently organise and lead virtual teams by knowing the key success factors and the virtual team members' needs.

What Participants are Expected to Do

Participation is fully voluntary, and participants may withdraw from research at any time without affecting their position, treatment or care.

The study starts with a group discussion about the topic. Then, each participant will be interviewed while guaranteeing the full confidentiality of the information, meaning all records containing personal information will remain confidential and no information which could lead to identification of any individual will be released.

Email Distribution

The researcher will take every care to remove responses from any identifying material as early as possible. Likewise individuals' responses will be kept confidential by the researcher and not be identified in the reporting of the research. However the researcher cannot guarantee the confidentiality or anonymity of material transferred by email or the internet.

Interview and Group Discussion Data Collection and Storage

The interview and focus group conversations will be audio-taped in order to be transcribed for the data analysis. A neutral XYZ internal person (without contact to participants) will transcribe the data. The participants' identity will be masked (e.g. the transcript will not contain names, but will be structured like "person A said"). Once transcribed, the audio-taped data will be deleted and the transcript will become the raw data, stored for seven years at XYZ.

Appendix B: Semi-Structured Interview Questions

University of South Australia

International Graduate School
of Business

Semi-Structured Interview Questions

Study Title	Study Conducted by
Managing Virtual Teams: A Case Study at XYZ Europe	Beat A. Buhlmann

- Questions might be refined or other questions might be added based on the results of research phase one (observation phase and group discussion).

- The information in brackets serves as refinement/additional trigger in case the initial question did not create enough data in the participant's response.

TERMINOLOGY AND CHANGE TO VIRTUAL TEAMS
What does "virtual team" mean to you? (What does "team" and what does "virtual" mean to you?)

Tell me how you experienced the reorganisation in February 2003 which lead to geographically dispersed virtual teams at XYZ Europe.

What do you miss compared to the situation before February 2003, meaning compared to the time with local marketing teams?

How did the change to virtual teams impact your
- working style/behaviour?
- working efficiency?
- team spirit?
- overall happiness at work?

COMMUNICATION
Let's talk about communication

What have you experienced working with people with different native languages, but all speaking English? (Language barrier, misunderstandings...)

How does your communication with local employees differ from your communication with virtual team members? (way of communication, tools, speed, efficiency, quality…)

What are your top 3 communication problems you have experienced working in a virtual teams?

How would you try to fix them and why?

Let's talk about
- Use of email
- Use of Instant messenger
- Use of phone conferences
- Face-to-Face meetings

TRUST
Let's talk about trust. What does "trust" mean to you in your working environment?

What do you think about trust in virtual teams compared to local teams?

Can trust be built faster in local teams?

How do you build trust?

Let's talk about initial trust (the researcher might explain this term if needed)

Tell me about your experiences of no longer having a local manager any more.

MOTIVATION
What do you think about "Isolation in Virtual Teams"? (The researcher might explain this term if needed)

How can a manager or another team member motivate you remotely?

CULTURAL DIFFERENCES
What cultural differences have you experienced working in a virtual team? (Working style, communication, punctuality, work speed, work quality…)

How do you get along with these differences?

Do you adapt your behaviour according to the person's cultural background? If yes, how?

What about virtual team literature or courses?

PERSONAL WORK PATTERNS
The participant will be presented with what the researcher discovered during the observation phase and group discussion (phase 1 of the DBA project). The findings are discussed.

Appendix C: Node Structure after Coding

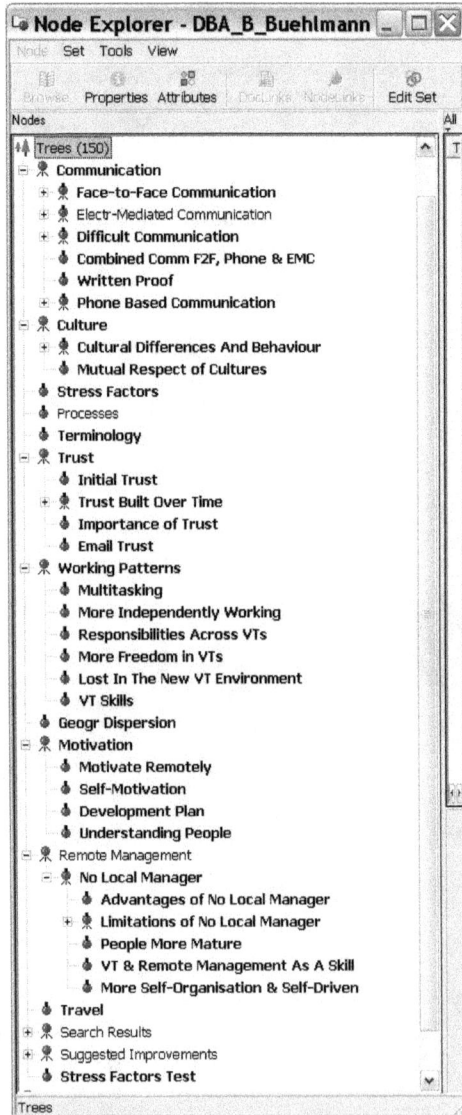

Node Explorer - DBA_B_Buehlmann

Node Set Tools View

Browse Properties Attributes DocLinks NodeLinks Edit Set

Nodes   All

- Trees (150)
  - Communication
    - Face-to-Face Communication
    - Electr-Mediated Communication
    - Difficult Communication
    - Combined Comm F2F, Phone & EMC
    - Written Proof
    - Phone Based Communication
  - Culture
    - Cultural Differences And Behaviour
    - Mutual Respect of Cultures
  - Stress Factors
  - Processes
  - Terminology
  - Trust
    - Initial Trust
    - Trust Built Over Time
    - Importance of Trust
    - Email Trust
  - Working Patterns
    - Multitasking
    - More Independently Working
    - Responsibilities Across VTs
    - More Freedom in VTs
    - Lost In The New VT Environment
    - VT Skills
  - Geogr Dispersion
  - Motivation
    - Motivate Remotely
    - Self-Motivation
    - Development Plan
    - Understanding People
  - Remote Management
    - No Local Manager
      - Advantages of No Local Manager
      - Limitations of No Local Manager
      - People More Mature
      - VT & Remote Management As A Skill
      - More Self-Organisation & Self-Driven
  - Travel
  - Search Results
  - Suggested Improvements
  - Stress Factors Test

Trees

Appendix D: Comparison of Original and Altered Model

Compelling Challenge

Time Differences

Lack of Casual,
Face-to-Face Contact
With Team Members

Lavish Information
Flow: Synchronous
& Asynchronous

Leader's Clarity
& Commitment

Jointly Defined
Identity, Goals &
Processes

Cultural
Differences

Pressure to Pursue
Local Priorities

Performance Management

Key
— (out) Centrifugal forces pulling the team apart
- - ► (in) Centripetal forces bringing the team together
Note: Arrow size indicates relative power of the force

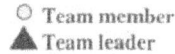

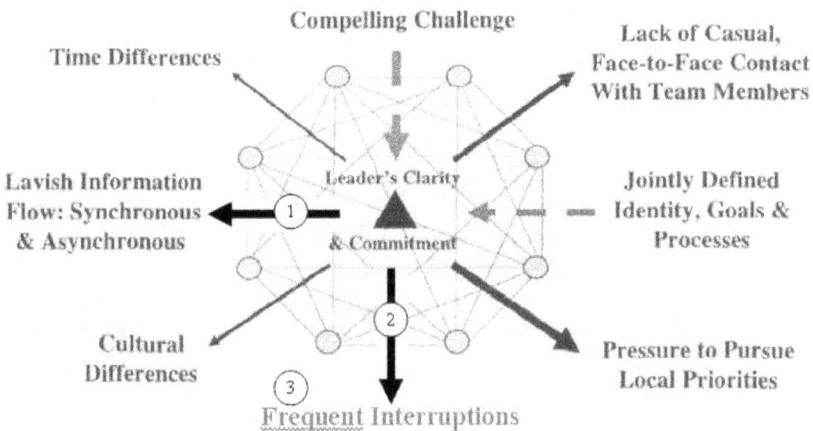

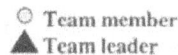

○ Team member
▲ Team leader

Compelling Challenge

Time Differences

Lack of Casual,
Face-to-Face Contact
With Team Members

Lavish Information
Flow: Synchronous
& Asynchronous

Leader's Clarity
& Commitment

Jointly Defined
Identity, Goals &
Processes

Cultural
Differences

Pressure to Pursue
Local Priorities

Frequent Interruptions

Key
— (out) Centrifugal forces pulling the team apart
- - ► (in) Centripetal forces bringing the team together
Note: Arrow size indicates relative power of the force

○ Team member
▲ Team leader

Appendix E: Listing of all Findings

Finding 1:   In general, virtual team members at XYZ Europe do not link difficulty of communication to the use of a common language (English).

Finding 2:   Most interviewees encountered more difficulties communicating with French colleagues.

Finding 3:   In a virtual team environment, FTF communication seems to be of vital importance.

Finding 4:   However, FTF requires travel. Besides the high cost, the time impact on the employees' lives does not seem to be taken into consideration sufficiently.

Finding 5:   A FTF meeting with all team members seems to be needed as early as possible in a work relationship, preferably at the very beginning.

Finding 6:   Voice-based communication lacks a written record.

Finding 7:   Virtual team members seem to appreciate a written record after communicative interactions.

Finding 8:   Voice-based communication seems to reduce the likelihood of misunderstandings significantly.

Finding 9:   Voice-based communication should be applied to resolve conflicts quickly.

Finding 10:   Most virtual team members experience difficulties dealing with the considerable volume of emails.

Finding 11:   Most virtual team members were not aware of the number of emails they send on a daily basis.

Finding 12:   The sender of an email loses control over the message and its future utilisation.

Finding 13:   Emails may cause a conflict of responsibility.

Finding 14:   Most virtual team members struggle with prioritisation in regard to the amount of emails.

Finding 15:   Alvesson & Deetz's concepts intended to create a critical research environment could be applied and appear to be functional.

Finding 16:   In a virtual business environment, the cardinal feature of IM is its ability to indicate which team members are online and therefore reachable.

Finding 17:   Most virtual team members exchange rather brief messages via IM.

Finding 18:   IM permits contacting team members more quickly and at lower cost compared to the phone.

Finding 19: To improve virtual team interactions, an official code of conduct for each communication channel should be applied.

Finding 20: Virtual team members often combine communication channels. The most frequent combinations of communication channels are email-phone and email-IM.

Finding 21: Overall, there seems to be a mainly inversely proportional relationship between the team members' preference of a communication channel and the frequency a channel is used.

Finding 22: Most virtual team members were not aware of the existence of initial trust, but eventually quickly came to acknowledge that is was something important and valuable.

Finding 23: Early FTF interactions, even if not job-related, may facilitate the virtual team members' trust building process.

Finding 24: In virtual teams, living up to agreed expectations may facilitate the trust building process even without FTF interaction.

Finding 25: People executing trust-building measures should think about whether trust can be built by mechanical methods or whether trust needs to be earned by the other person. If trust needs to be earned, trust-building measures might need to be adapted.

Finding 26: In early stages of a virtual team's life, FTF or phone-based communication seems to be preferable to EMC.

Finding 27:   The virtual team environment seems to require team members
                with a specific virtual team skill set (more mature, better
                organised, better structured, and independent working style).

Finding 28:   Companies might think about adapting their recruiting process
                when hiring new virtual team members.

Finding 29:   Overall, most interviewees disrelished multitasking.

Finding 30:   Tuckman's stage model has proved itself and could be connected
                to the existence of task-based trust.

Finding 31:   In most instances, the Virtual Team Dynamics model could be
                confirmed by the findings of this study. However, three
                alterations were made in order to reflect and incorporate findings
                11, 27, 28, and 29.

www.ingramcontent.com/pod-product-compliance
Lightning Source LLC
Chambersburg PA
CBHW061326220326
41599CB00026B/5047